THE FINEST ROOMS

IN FRANCE

THE FINEST ROOMS IN FRANCE

By the Editors of the French *House & Garden*

A Studio Book

THE VIKING PRESS

New York

LES NOUVELLES RÉUSSITES DE LA DÉCORATION FRANÇAISE
© 1966 by Les Éditions Condé Nast S.A. and Éditions Robert Laffont
THE FINEST ROOMS IN FRANCE
English translation Copyright 1967 in all countries of the International Copyright Union by The Viking Press, Inc.

First published in 1967 by The Viking Press, Inc.
625 Madison Avenue, New York, N.Y. 10022

Published simultaneously in Canada by
The Macmillan Company of Canada Limited

Printed and bound in France

By the editors of MAISON & JARDIN,
Paris, under the direction of

THOMAS KERNAN

Reporting by

**LA DUCHESSE D'AYEN
GEORGES DUBOIS
JACQUELINE DE LÉON**

Text by

SOUREN MELIKIAN

Designed by

PAUL MARIONNET

Photographs by

JACQUES BOUCHER
Jacques Bachmann, Frank Beyda, R. Emmett Bright
Jean-Jacques Bugat, Anthony Denney, F. Fâh
Marc Garanger, Grigsby, Gérard Guillat
André Kertesz, Alix de Preux, Danny Wann

Drawings by

Denise Nicollet, Olivier Mourgue, Daniel Delmotte, Pascal Mourgue

Production by

Hervé Gyssels, Édouard Grillot

Translation by

PAUL H. BONNER, JR.

Contents

A COUNTRY BOUQUET

SMALL PARIS APARTMENTS

PROBLEMS AND SOLUTIONS

GLOSSARY OF STYLES

INDEX

Ever since the arts and industries of France ceased to suffer from the scarcities created by World War II, *House & Garden'*s sister magazine, *Maison & Jardin,* has been the faithful reporter and interpreter of the decoration of French homes. This book, which, for the main part, shows antiques in contemporary settings, is based on material published, in Paris, by *Maison & Jardin* in the last five years.

It is pleasant to portray this period, for though it is brief, it has coincided with an era of extraordinary prosperity for France. Trade, invention, social progress, international influence, all these have again made France one of Europe's richest countries. Whenever this affluence occurred previously, it witnessed a corresponding flowering of all the creative arts. But today this certainly, and unfortunately, is not true. In painting, we see no new Renoir or Matisse on the horizon, in sculpture no Maillol or Rodin, in music no Debussy or Ravel, and in the domain of interior decoration no Jacob or Majorelle. We discern no style of the Fifth Republic (or, as the wits would have it, no "style Charles XI").

Thus the decoration of the past decade is a synthesis of period styles, drawn from the repertory of the last three hundred years. Contemporary furniture of the international school, but seldom of French origin, has gained a wide acceptance in offices, cafés, and public places. But in the home this is not so. The Frenchman and even more the French woman have remained rigorously conservative.

Even period decoration is subject to constant change, and no one, except in a museum, seeks the exact replica of a historic room. In addition, each generation interprets a given style in its own fashion; the Louis XVI, as revived in the early days of our century, is not at all the Louis XVI as seen by the decorator to day. And it is not necessary to wait a generation: the alert critic can clearly distinguish a room decorated in 1955 from one created in 1966 even when the two are inspired by the same historic theme.

First of all, there are constant changes in colors. The billiard green and "suspender" red which enlivened the immediate post-war years have been consigned to limbo. (The Paris decorators called these colors English, although London never saw them except in a Highlander's tartans!) The immediate successors, in the 1950s, a gamut of cold blues and greens, have in turn given way to a vibrant palette which is audacious without being vulgar. We find pistachio, linden, almond for the greens, turquoise and kingfisher for the blues; we also find ocher and mustard, rust, and pomegranate. Even the accent colors have a kind of Oriental mystery.

As far as the furniture itself is concerned, the limited appeal of contemporary designs has already been suggested. This does not mean that a great deal of modern furniture, imported from Scandinavia and Italy, or copies of their models, is not sold by department stores to young couples about to furnish their nests in one of the great apartment-house complexes now beginning to ring French cities. But the use of this furniture is, on the whole, a simple matter of placing, with little research that could aspire to the term "decoration."

In the decorator's field, the favorite of the last few years is the "Haute Epoque," that is to say, the furniture styles of the century prior to Louis XV. Since typical furniture of the Louis XIV period was rather elaborate, "Haute Epoque" is really closer to the Louis XIII style, made in non-veneered native woods and without decoration or carving. Very few pieces, of course, date back to the 17th century itself, but since much provincial furniture was made as late as the 19th century in a survival of the style, and since in Spain its manufacture continues to this day, it is not surprising to find so many "Haute Epoque" pieces gracing French country houses and the high-ceilinged rooms of remodeled city houses.

English furniture has also had its vogue in France. What is interesting is that French decorators, combing the flotsam and jetsam of Chelsea and Portobello Road, have chosen not the classic Sheraton and Chippendale pieces, but furniture and *objets d'art* immediately preceding the Victorian era. Original, sometimes romantic and comfortable pieces —as only the English know how to make them—fit well into the apartments of Paris.

The disposition of furniture within the room has also seen changes. The solemn circle of chairs facing the fireplace which was the hallmark of the French salon has been broken up into separate groups—so much so that in this book a series of pages has been devoted to the "conversation corner."

Fabrics have never been more splendid. Although one may see less than one used to of that most classic of prints, the simple toile de Jouy, all other types of printed fabrics from the repertory of the early 1800s seem more plentiful, their colors reinterpreted in new tones of the day. Above all, a new dimension has been added by innovations both in weaving and embossing fabrics, and also in the use of heavy fibers such as hemp with linen, and the outer cocoon in the spinning of silk. Only during the past decade have synthetic and artificial fibers gained wide acceptance in France, and while they may look the same as traditional fabrics, these new materials have proved more practical in many ways.

The individual object is all-important today, and the passion for collecting and combining sometimes quite unrelated things defies any attempt at classification. Artifacts of all periods have been retrieved from the garret and placed on the salon table. The well-worn tool of a long-dead artisan may stand beside a bronze or a porcelain; the animal and vegetable kingdoms too have been plundered for their most curious and evocative forms. But a subtle art is involved in the juxtaposition of a diversity of objects, and interior designers and hostesses enjoy making their own improvisations.

The reason that the lady of the house can be spoken of in the same breath as the professional decorator is that an important phenomenon of the past ten years has been the remarkable increase in public interest and knowledge in everything that concerns interior design. A great deal of education and familiarization by magazines, by the movies and the daily press, has awakened the interest of whole sections of society—people to whom a few years ago decoration was an unknown world. At the same time, among the privileged families where good taste has long been a tradition, the knowledge of specialized fields of the arts is sometimes remarkable, and many of these amateurs have shared with the professionals in the general enlivenment of decorative art. Perhaps this has tended to be derivative rather than truly creative, but it has been practiced with such high standards and refinement that the French home can again be said to express an almost perfect combination of beauty and comfort, using traditional means in a graceful and contemporary way.

THOMAS KERNAN,

Editor of *Maison & Jardin*

GRAND DECORATION
Parisian apartments

**At the entrance,
bold colors**

The inspiration for this small entrance hall came from some of the exquisite apartments in the Ducal Palace at Urbino. The exotic veneers and embossed velvet remind one of a Renaissance coffer and give the hall a sumptuous quality. The effect does not depend on any given style. The guiding principles here, and on the following pages, were the use of bold contrasting colors and of very clear angles and lines.

THE SIGNIFICANCE
OF ORNAMENTS
In the manner
of the "Haute Epoque"

Present-day decorators love the "Haute Epoque," with its vertical flights, bare stone, and generally rugged quality — but they also like the comfort of soft sofas. In this spirit, yet defying any definite classification of style, is Carlos Ortiz Cabrera's décor for the two upper floors of this unusual house facing the apse of Notre-Dame. Cabrera's solution to the problem represents a triumph of organization. Previously this house was a strange museum of stone, created between 1920 and 1930, containing casements and gargoyles from Gothic churches. In order to keep the Gothic mood, the stonework was cleaned, and the wood surfaces, as well as the stone and marble floors, were brought back into good condition. No wallpaper or figured fabrics were used. But as a slavish copy of an early style was not intended, the designer brought together such diverse objects as modern andirons designed by Metcalf, a fantastic German medieval chandelier, and a marble bust of the Renaissance period. The unique selection and arrangement of pieces also includes a Louis XIII gaming table, a Louis XIII chair with Hungarian embroidery on the silk cover, Hiquily sculpture, a pair of animals copied from Nevers pottery (asymmetrically placed so as to be appreciated as works of art instead of mere decorative pieces), and a 17th-century Savonnerie rug with a black background.

Objects had to be spaced out so that they did not compete with one another, and thus the effect is one of moderation. The central design theme established for the house is the continual use of asymmetric arrangements. Right angles abound — around the sofa, in the front hall beside the staircase, around the canopied bed — and the eye is always led to some object or ornament arranged as a center of interest.

▲
Through the Gothic window — fitted into the roofing by the previous owner — a beautiful view of Paris, with the cathedral in the foreground, can be enjoyed.

◄ **In the hall, the use of many rhythmic lines is most dramatic. Although the décor is somewhat spread out, unity has been successfully achieved between the twisted medieval column, the banisters on the staircase, the wrought-iron stabile by Hiquily, and the black Louis XIV table.**

Many periods are combined in the great living room. The Flemish tapestry dates from the 15th century, the gaming table is Louis XIII, the gilt wood armchair in the foreground is Louis XIV, the other chair is Louis XV, and the coffee table, made of a stucco tabletop with legs by Harald Cousins, is half classic, half contemporary. The repetition of vertical lines gives the room unity. The stunning bracket by Auguste Fix seems to accentuate the folds of the draperies, and the abstract sculpture by Cousins breaks up into long vertical lines which are repeated by the folds of the curtains.

At the end of the living room, all purely decorative notions have been avoided. The walls around the great fireplace have been painted to resemble white stone, and against this background a Roman bust of the Italian Renaissance is most attractively displayed. On the floor, the Savonnerie carpet with its black background provides an unusual contrast with the pattern of the marble. The Louis XIV armchair, covered in velvet of the period, stands alone as something to be admired. Only Metcalf's bronze andirons have been placed symmetrically in this unique décor.

Decorating
with
works of art

The play of light and shadow accentuates the contours of the room. The angled sofa lends an air of warmth and comfort, and the 17th-century Dutch landscape is both fitting and majestic in its simplicity.

The unusual ornament is perhaps the main theme of this end of the living room, which doubles as a dining area. The tabletop, resting on oak legs, is a mosaic of polychrome marble, composed predominantly of greens and reds. Over the center of it hangs a wrought-iron chandelier, and on the wall behind it are two paintings by the Hungarian artist Hantai, placed on either side of a Venetian mirror. The sofa, covered with doeskin in an elephant-hide shade, adds another unusual touch of texture and color.

A handsome staircase leads up to a gallery. Instead of traditional carpeting, the oak treads, held in place by black iron rods, are covered in cowhide, which is a very pleasant material to walk on.

In Paris, near Notre-Dame

A simple corner of the 16th-century gallery was made into a small and intimate library. Its warm colors are very suitable since it is a room reserved for evening use. The shantung-covered sofa has bright cushions, and an exotic note is introduced by the Japanese lacquer chest and the 19th-century bronze ibis, also of Japanese origin.

Varying schemes
to brighten special rooms

The design of the bedroom was strengthened by ▶ the use of contrasting rectangles and curves. On the walls, the 15th-century linenfold panelling was refurbished and waxed to give it the same honey color as the beams. The Louis XIII stool was covered with a solid velvet to emphasize the forceful architecture. The only purely decorative notes are the appliqués designed by Metcalf, but even these were treated like an architectural frieze on the linen canopy.   ▼

◀ This small sitting room was designed as a retreat for the owner's wife. The rather severe architecture was softened by the use of quiet colors, and by the choice of romantic paintings and 18th-century furniture. On the red tile floor are two Oriental rugs, and the ceiling between the light-colored oak beams is a lovely turquoise blue. A sculptured panel, dating from the Renaissance, was the key to the design of the stonework which surrounds the fireplace. Over this hangs a triptych composed of three flower paintings. The angled sofa was upholstered in a blue and cream checked taffeta, and striped Genoese velvet in the same colors was used for the Louis XVI armchair. On the walls, covered in greige cotton, are witches' mirrors in different sizes, with flower pictures and landscapes. The curtains at the window are tobacco-brown.

ROYAL ERAS REVIVED
The connoisseur's display case

◄ **Symmetry on a grand scale distinguishes the halls. Two classic-shaped niches frame the door, but they have an air of lightness which is due to the consoles under them, and to the pair of tall wooden tulip holders carved and painted to imitate Delft pottery.**

The first impression one receives on entering this apartment, decorated by Georges Geffroy, is its rare and precious quality. In the sitting room, the feeling springs from the luster of the gold-striped velvet and from the 18th-century bas-relief, with a frame carved to resemble twisting leaves that climb from curve to curve almost to the ceiling. It is hard to believe that the apartment is in the 16th Arrondissement, for there is none of the usual distinguished anonymity or standardized elegance. Equally interesting is the décor of the dining room. Here, a blue and white Mongolian rug was chosen, together with a porcelain stove (set in a niche in the Louis XV manner), and a Chinese wallpaper that dominates the entire room. The bedroom is more simply decorated, yet the ingenious use of heavy velvet, stretching from the cornice to the baseboard and pierced by a vast circular window, gives the room quite fantastic proportions.

We are often led to ask what it is that gives any successful decorating scheme its sense of absolute rightness. To some extent this is achieved through a proper respect for the architecture of the house and, more specifically, of each individual room. Georges Geffroy's style is to make "opening announcements" that give an immediate impression. In the front hall, the classical columns that frame the entrance to a sitting room of average proportions give strength to the décor and introduce the element of great architecture. In the dining room, the Chinese mural paper which is mounted like panelling, and, in the living room, the marble columns surmounted by urns, also give strength to these settings. Geffroy's use of green velvet in the living room is also exciting; he uses not just a small patch of it, but a great expanse that covers the walls right up to the cornice, and over it. In contrast to this warm background are the coldness of the marble and the hard brilliance of brass and tortoise-shell Boulle marquetry. The room is uncluttered, yet it has a feeling of great richness, due to the princely quality of the Régence mirror and the Boulle bookcase. Louis XIV pieces are mixed with those of the Louis XV and Louis XVI periods, and the velvet walls are typical of the Romantic era. The total result is the triumph of an art lover who has combined various collectors' items into a décor that is perfectly designed for elegant present-day entertaining.

▲
The surprise comes at the end. Set on their marble bases, two covered Louis XVI urns, worthy of Versailles, punctuate a perspective that is in the best classic manner. But from archway to archway, the eye is carried to the immense and unusual false window at the end.

◄ **Two antique-looking columns set the style at the threshold of the sitting room, but the decoration is as uncluttered as the opening statement is solemn. The walls are painted to imitate marble. Nothing competes with the one strong note : the bas-relief of carved wood in its graceful, gilded, Louis XV frame.**

On the avenue Foch, dramatic echoes of China

◀ The blond, white, and blue dining room is covered with a 17th-century Chinese wallpaper originally designed for the English market. The lively and very rare panels are framed by borders, most of them antique, in a bamboo pattern. The blue 18th-century Mongolian carpet is a rarity also. The double curtains of East Indian raw silk are parted by tasselled tiebacks and reveal banana-yellow curtains. The white doors are painted with trompe l'œil moldings, heightened by thin gold stripes. The Regency table, the blue and white Louis XV chairs upholstered in blue damask, the carved wooden English console tables of the same period, and the stove of Nancy porcelain all combine to give a true feeling of the 18th century, regardless of their origin.

The pantry has glass panels resembling facets of a prism. Here bowls of flowers are arranged for use ▶ later on the dining room table. Raw Thai silk is stretched behind the glass to supply a bright note in this attractively delicate color scheme.

Beautiful furniture
creates the atmosphere.

▲
The harmonies of metal and velvet lend brilliance to the living
room and make it sparkling yet understated, formal yet almost
intimate. A glass-enclosed bookcase of Boulle marquetry, one
of the most beautiful pieces of furniture that the Louis XIV era
produced, is displayed like a jewel against the velvet.

◀ Even the least significant pieces of furniture and ornamentation
take on new importance against this mellow, antique background,
from the filing cabinet, whose delicate design would otherwise
be lost, to the Louis XV folding table. The gilt bronze sconces
from the at Château of Champs shed a soft glow on the velvet.

Several masterpieces at once catch the eye: the gilded wood ▶
Régence mirror, the great Persian carpet of the Safawid era that
was originally ordered for a King of Poland, and, in the middle
of the room, the four-sided Régence table which displays a Greek
sketch for an icon. The contrasts in proportion are most artful,
such as the mirror frame that overlaps the cornice, the little
four-legged footstool in front of the fireplace, and the children's
armchairs that stand next to the table.

Even the least important areas were treated like difficult architectural problems. This little hall that leads from the bedroom to the bathroom has wall covering and portières in red, a color popular in the days of Charles X.

◄ **In remodeling the bedroom the problem was to reduce the excessive length of the room without sacrificing space. By the building of an arcade at one end, two closets were created which eliminated the need for large pieces of furniture and also improved the shape of the room. Between the closets, an oversize bronze Directoire bed was placed. The black wooden pilasters are as slim as the bars on the bedstead. On the rear wall, braid decorates the red fabric and emphasizes the vertical line. Two white plaster medallions on black backgrounds — Chopin and Schubert, the owner's favorite composers — accent this triumphal arch.**

Above right : The wallpaper used for the front hall makes it appear twice its former length. The light blue paper, with gold and black veining, and the white painted woodwork, create a charming trompe l'œil. The vase on the small table makes a focal point for the ingeniously created perspective.

The least promising-looking quarters can be made into something beautiful, even an apartment in a modern building where the proportions are usually uninteresting and the doors and windows are apt to be awkwardly placed. An example is this ninth-floor apartment in a building on the rue Docteur-Blanche which is occupied by the composer Baron de Banfield. The decorator used cornices to help rectify the ungainly dimensions. The windows had to stay where they were, but she moved all the doors and spirited away a neon-lighted beam which separated the living room from the study. The living room presented problems that confront all first occupants of new buildings, and we see here how a major defect was turned into an asset. Madeleine Castaing chose the styles that were popular in Europe in 1830: Regency, Charles X, and Biedermeier. She brought back the columns and arcades that were typical of the period, and used them with the consummate skill on which her international reputation is based. Between the living room and the study she erected a light and graceful archway that covers the offending beam, separates the two areas without cutting down the feeling of openness, and creates a perspective of neo-classic inspiration. In each room she introduced cornices of English design to give more apparent height to the ceilings. By this clever means, a tiny entrance has been made to seem much larger, receding from arch to arch. Again, in the bedroom, the same effect — somewhere between true perspective and trompe l'œil — is created by placing the bed halfway into an alcove built into one end of the room. The whole apartment has an uncluttered look. The only very large pieces are the copper columns in the living room. The chairs are light and slender, and the graceful tables appear smaller than they actually are on the wall-to-wall carpeting. Echoes of classicism blend, like fleeting memories, with delightful touches of soaring romanticism.

VIEWS OF EUROPE, 1830
An apartment redecorated by Madeleine Castaing

Indoor architecture
can transform modern floor plans

◀ **Trompe l'œil dominates the music room where a panoramic Italian painting of the 17th century, which belonged at one time to the town hall of Trieste, is mounted as a single panel. The very real copper Regency column in the foreground enhances the simulated perspective of the painting. The sinuous curves of the baby grand piano lead the eye to the imaginary vanishing point. The lightness of the caned English chairs that date from the beginning of the 19th century goes well in a room that has the unplanned look of the stage in a concert hall.**

A portico in the Regency manner made it possible to ▶ camouflage an awkward beam and, at the same time, divide an overly large room into a well-balanced "suite". The mahogany of the bookcase and the English desk strikes a strong color note against the pastel tones, and the portrait of Rossini recalls the fact that this is the home of an operatic composer, and one of Italian stock.

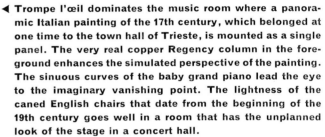

◀ **Like a stage set of 1830, the windows of the living room are hung with garnet curtains of plain silk edged with stamped velvet borders and lined with black velvet. Drawn back, they seem to reveal an alcove furnished with a banquette, but in actual fact the radiators are here, hidden by the same material that is used to cover the walls of the room, a fabric of white, light blue and dark blue stripes.**

A light, spacious, high-ceilinged apartment, with wide windows overlooking the Bois de Boulogne. The generous 19th-century architectural proportions are a later version of Louis XVI. The young owners wished to display their fine possessions in a setting reminiscent of the 18th century, which was a period they greatly admired. To try to re-create the period exactly was out of the question, for the rooms had low wainscoting decorated with molding, small wall areas, plaster cornices, and other details typical of the Third Republic. Instead, Delbée, of the firm of Jansen, borrowed ideas from several recent styles. He used areas of brocade and pickled the wall panelling almost white in the style that was popular in the era of "Arts-Déco." He brought together the finest antiques — a clock made for Stanislas Leczinski, a chest of drawers bearing Roussel's stamp— and added reproductions to create a new 18th-century look with a masterpiece dominating each room. In the living room, the Goya portrait is the focal point. The painting, which still has its original carved and gilded wood frame, is displayed against a dove-gray, silk velvet wall covering, which is repeated in the curtains. Dominating the bedroom is the portrait by Mme. Vigée-Lebrun which is centered in the alcove. In the dining room, with its refurbished English Georgian panelling, an 18th-century Sèvres service inspired the decoration. In each room subtle harmonies were created so that each masterpiece looked perfectly at home in its setting. The patterns of foliage and flowers, borrowed from the 19th century as well as the 18th, bring to mind the fact that this is an appropriate décor for a young couple — friendly and devoid of any kind of museum-like rigidity.

The brocade and the painting were the starting point for the decoration. The brocade, a square of flowers against two shades of gold, is let into the panelling and creates a frame for Mme Vigée-Lebrun's portrait of Marie-Antoinette and her children. The gilding on the Louis XVI furniture repeats highlights of the brocade. In keeping with the subtle color scheme, the bookcases were pickled almost white.

◄ French and English 18th-century styles are closely linked in the dining room. The green and white Sèvres service, the principal ornament, inspired the display cases in the Adam manner. They appear as if they were supported by the two semi-circular Adam console tables that are in the best tradition of English cabinetmaking. The Swedish crystal chandelier also has an English look.

THE 18TH CENTURY
ON THE AVENUE FOCH
Under the eye of Goya

A painting,
a piece of furniture,
and Sèvres china
set the theme.

▲
Flowers and foliage luxuriate in this bedroom, which has an air of gentility in the Louis XV manner. The antique panelling has white details against a pale rose background, and opens on an alcove lined with the same blue damask that covers the bed and the chairs. The focal point is Mme. Vigée-Lebrun's portrait of her daughter.

◄ Goya's "Young Girl with a Rose" set the color scheme and determined the choice of fabrics in the living room. The continuous valance running around the top of the dove-gray silk velvet walls is in matching shades, and the blue in the painting is repeated in the pale blue damask used for the Régence sofa and chair coverings. The Savonnerie rug is reminiscent of those in the Royal Palace at La Granja. The magnificent gilt-bronze sconces repeat the gold tone of the picture frames. This room, like the others, was planned so that each masterpiece has its own uncluttered space. The marquetry of the commode and the Guardi landscape stand out brilliantly against the wall space between two of the windows.

VIRTUOSITY
IN A 20TH-CENTURY APARTMENT

Sliding panelled doors
are an asset.

▲
With all its doors closed, the living room takes on proportions that are closer to the 18th century than they are to modern architecture. The two panels are carved with Louis XV motifs and painted blue to match the panelling, so that there is nothing to show that they are mounted on tracks (see page 291) and can therefore disappear to join the living and dining rooms.

The old-fashioned front hall (above right) is traditional. Only the colors depart from the strict canon: the rose and white marble flooring, and the gray and gold veining on the dado, cornice and molding. The silk shantung portières of Directoire green are pulled back to reveal a glimpse of the apartment, and a corner of an 18th-century landscape with classical ruins. The folding chairs and the bronze Directoire chandelier pinpoint the style chosen for this front hall.

The virtuosity that Victor Grandpierre displayed in M. and Mme. Louis François-Poncet's apartment in a new building on the Avenue Foch is doubly interesting. From a practical point of view, it shows how the ingenious use of sliding doors can make it possible to vary the size of a room, and, aesthetically, it proves that 18th-century decoration can be quite at home in a modern apartment which features an entire wall of glass. Obviously no attempt could be made at reconstructing the 18th century exactly, yet a feeling of that period, and of luxury and comfort, was intended. To begin with, Grandpierre tried to correct the boxy aspect of the rooms. The living room walls were covered with Louis XV panelling, and the floor was surfaced with a parquet copied from Versailles. Largely for reasons of comfort, two contemporary sofas that have nothing to do with Louis XV were placed face to face on either side of the fireplace — an idea borrowed from Victorian England. Between these is a modern coffee table, and the whole conversation area is set off by a rug of latticework design.

All the colors are light and fresh: blue and cream for the panelling, honey color for the sofas. When necessary, the sliding doors between the living and dining rooms can disappear into the walls to create a large, modern open space, or they can be closed to make two entirely separate rooms. Everywhere advantage was taken of the main basic asset: a generous amount of space. In the front hall, an additional air of spaciousness was created with the help of checkerboard flooring. The almost theatrical proportions justify the large draperies, which are tied back to reveal the fine décor.

◄ **Although the dining room (opposite) is in the late 18th-century tradition, it differs only slightly from a typical Second Empire room. At most the window area is too big, and to cope with this problem Grandpierre cut it down with very useful, angled, built-in cabinets. A cornice with modillions helps to** give a classic air to the architecture. Otherwise, simplicity is the keynote: yellow shantung for the walls and curtains, white molding picked out with gold to match the sliding doors. On the walls, a framed piece of Restoration wallpaper and some Charles X gouaches give additional character to the room.

A window wall framed by panelling

▲
When the sliding doors disappear into the narrow slots behind the panelling, the living and dining room areas make a single great sweep of space. Both floors are covered with identical rugs made out of strips of broadloom. These rugs established a basis for the symmetrical arrangements on both sides of the door.

◄ With the sliding doors closed, smaller panels open like ordinary double doors between the living room and dining room.

Antique Louis XV panelling gives the living room its air of authenticity. In keeping ▶ with the period is the floral design of the silk curtains, which echoes the design of the broadloom rug, patterned after a Savonnerie. The 19th-century sofas covered in raw silk — one bigger than the other to keep the arrangement from being too pat — have a true bourgeois solidity. The tiger-striped velvet on the Louis XVI stool evokes the splendors of the Second Empire, and the two oval paintings on the wall introduce a romantic note, reiterated by the lotus-green chairs on the terrace. But the caned Louis XV chairs near the fireplace, and the velvet-covered Louis XVI love seat, help to keep the 18th century dominant.

ECHOES OF LOUIS XVI
With an air of intimacy

Purity of color is the principal charm of the dining room. The blond tobacco-color chosen for the painted walls and the ribbed velvet curtains is framed by the white moldings and cornice. The shirred, teal blue faille of the screen, which is set into mahogany stretchers, contrasts with the somber antique velvet of the chairs.

Like a velvet-lined jewel box, the front hall has walls of ribbed velvet in the same moss green as the carpet. All the furniture here is mahogany — the English cabinet, the mirror, and the chairs by Georges Jacob — limiting the basic palette of the room to two colors. The chairs are upholstered in black horsehair, and on the cabinet a celadon vase in a Louis XVI mounting of gilt bronze strikes a brilliant note of gold.

In the bedroom, the fabrics run a gamut of color from greige to black, producing ▶ an unusually soothing effect. The panelling and the ottoman rib curtains are in pale beige, the velvet on the bed is in raw sienna, and the armchairs have black horsehair. The room derives its unity as much from the colors and the materials as from the style. All the furniture here is mahogany, which is a very unusual wood for chairs of the Louis XVI period.

In this small and lovely apartment the color scheme depends largely on neutral tones. Everything is exquisitely muted: pale 18th-century water colors in frames of faded gold, embossed velvet in various shades of brown, and curtains in subtle colors and shades. The furniture, mostly mahogany with a few painted chairs, has a familiar look. Serge and Anne Royaux have ingeniously arranged the décor to create the atmosphere of a rediscovered old house. Suddenly, while musing in front of one of the charming chairs, one realizes that its lyre-back can only be the work of Georges Jacob, and that almost everything in the apartment is of museum caliber.

In the living room are three shades of beige: in the panelling, in the ottoman rib of the sofa, and in the velvet. The mood of the room is so relaxing that it is almost an effort to appreciate fully the set of water colors of Italian architecture by Percier, Fontaine, and Clérisseau, or to notice that the modest mahogany candlestand near the fireplace is a signed piece by Canabas. One has the same feeling in the dining room, where the blond tobacco-color of the painted walls and the ribbed velvet curtains nearly camouflages the lovely Louis XVI furniture. The subtle effect of the decoration is even more overwhelming in the bedroom. The arrangement of the antique carved mahogany Louis XVI bed and chairs (of extraordinary rarity) seems totally unself-conscious. Everything has been most carefully planned, however, and the success of the room is largely due to the choice of colors: greige panelling, raw sienna velvet on the bed, and the brown mahogany — made darker by the shadows of the carvings. The subtle gradation culminates in the black horsehair upholstery of the fine armchairs. The result shows the taste of a great collector who has always lived with old family pieces but who never insists on showing off their splendors in too grand a manner.

Variations of beige appear throughout the living room. An extraordinary modulation of shades and materials gives a feeling of richness to the walls. The cornice and the moldings have a faint touch of rose, which contrasts with the greige of the rest of the wood. In the same way, the rose silk of the undercurtains accents the pale beige of the ottoman rib draperies. This is the same ottoman rib used to cover the sofa, and, on the walls, it is bordered with rose-colored molding to create a muted background for a set of 18th-century water colors whose subtle tones would otherwise be overwhelmed. Everything in the room suggests, discreetly, that this is the home of a collector: the display table between the windows, a candlestand by Canabas next to the fireplace (above right), a sphere of Italian marble standing on the coffee table — made of a modern marble tabletop set on an antique 18th-century base for a chest — marble busts of emperors, and onyx obelisks. The minerals on the étagère also demonstrate the owners' passion for collecting.

An array of neutral shades

A PRINCELY INHERITANCE
Variety with unity

Prince Jean-Louis de Faucigny-Lucinge, President of the Cercle Interallié, is at the same time a devoted collector, an enlightened lover of modern art who likes to display it, and a prince who is faithful to family mementos. His varying possessions are perfectly combined in a décor that somehow manages to convey an extraordinary feeling of unity. In his new apartment on the sixth floor of a light, airy building on the Avenue Montaigne, the Prince wanted to have plenty of space and also a background that was suitable, yet out of the ordinary. The decoration was done by the architect Süe shortly after World War II, and it has stood up admirably through the years, with only a little repainting here and there.

The dining room walls were marbleized to create the right atmosphere for the massive furniture, some of which was in the "Return from Egypt" style. In the living room, the light butter-yellow matches one of the hues in the immense 19th-century Persian rug — a rug whose Surrealist cats have an irresistible charm for a collector who admires Dali. In the library, a warmer background shade was chosen for the display of innumerable medallions of the 18th and 19th centuries. Throughout the apartment, careful thought was given to the placement of the major items — items that are as important to decoration in the grand manner as the mark of a couturier is to a beautiful ball gown. Thus, in one close area, there is an antique Louis XV clock adorned with Chinese figures, framed by two candelabra; and in another one, a child's portrait by J. G. Guyp; and in yet another appropriate spot, a pair of Empire carytids that now support lamps.

◄ Family mementos are grouped in the library, in a clever arrangement that betrays the passions of a collector. Medallions that would be lost if each were displayed separately have been massed in a large niche, painted off-white to match the walls. Three sculptured profiles by Chinard dominate the scene. In the middle, twenty-eight white porcelain medallions in their black frame suggest amusing dialogues, and on either side are silhouettes of Prince and Princesse de Faucigny-Lucinge. Two panels, covered with garnet velvet, hold miniatures collected by the family throughout the 19th century.

▲ The dining room, with its formal but restful color scheme, was originally designed by the architect Süe. The beige-rose carpeting, combined with the different shades of gray in the pilasters and walls, re-creates a typical 18th-century palette. The colors soften the formality of the décor, as do the greige silk rep curtains with their orange and black trimming. An Oriental rug placed in the middle of the room gives it warmth. Even the massive late-18th-century furniture and the ''Return from Egypt'' sideboard do not interfere with the welcoming feeling of the room. The apartment is unmistakably that of a collector.

Beautiful objects
with space to breathe

Rare objects blended into a carefully worked out decorative theme give the living room its special quality—heavy, large-scale ones. An antique Louis XV gilt-framed mirror dominates a graceful sofa of the late 18th century, and a handsome "Return from Egypt" armchair stands next to a fragile candlestand. In the same way, the child's portrait by J. G. Guyp seems ready to overpower the little landscape by Dali, yet it does not. Lively figures give the decoration a Surrealist touch: the caryatid lamps on pedestals, the Queen Anne figures on either side of the fireplace, the little Dutch girl, the cats in the Persian rug.

THE CLASSIC STYLE UPDATED
The unexpected combined with the traditional

To start with, there was a vast apartment with an unsurpassed view of the Parc Monceau, and some rather formal and handsome furniture with the air of luxury that one would associate with a distinguished family. One might expect the combination of these two elements to produce a static and formal décor; but in the home of Raymond Guest, the American diplomat, and his wife, the former Princesse Caroline Murat, this danger was carefully avoided. Although attached to the mementos of her family, Mrs. Guest was also fully aware of present-day trends, and she looked for variations on the classic themes. To help solve the various decorating problems, she turned to the imaginative decorator Emilio Terry. In every room, the architecture, the doors, and the color scheme harmonize most happily, for the colors are gay and the shapes have clear outlines. But the decorator has often shaken the classic image with a bold stroke: in the anteroom, the sky-blue cupola is painted with clouds; in the front hall, an Aubusson of luminous colors contrasts with almost black portières; in the dining room, terra cotta is unexpectedly blended with green and blue. And in the main living room, which has great warmth despite the cold colors, the astonishing blue and white carpet in a geometric design is something that only a great decorator would have dared to use in such a room.

▲
The front hall is shaped like a long gallery cut off by nearly black, cotton satin portières. A pair of 19th-century Aubussons with fresh, strong colors — rose, green, and strawberry red — enliven the marbleized walls.

◄ Behind the second portière is a small anteroom, round as a drum. The walls are covered with ruby-red linen velvet, and the door, niches, and moldings are painted white with gold stripes. The cupola ceiling balances the elegant parquet floor. The design in exotic wood frames the mahogany and light-colored wood used at the center of the floor for the owners' initial.

The beauty of the dining room is derived partly from the ►
fine pure Regency furniture and partly from the imaginative decoration. All four walls are painted a matte terracotta, the cornice is white, and the antique-style frieze is gray-blue. Most unusual are the use of white for the door frames and moldings against the dark mahogany, and the introduction of black door handles.

A double door opens into a living room of imposing proportions. The gold and white door, cornice, and baseboard subtly blend with the 18th-century sconces, the fine gilt Louis XVI chairs, and the antique needlepoint. In the middle of the oblong room, a six-seated conversation piece from the Napoleon III era (it actually comes from Blenheim Palace) interposes its gilded wood and solid green velvet like a witty sally amidst the classic furnishings. The wide wall facing the three windows has been built out to make two niches with lowered, arched ceilings, suggesting alcoves. Small ornaments, placed around the room, make splashes of white: a Sèvres porcelain group, a "Woman Bathing" painted by Falconet, and small pieces of alabaster. A very fine embossed silk velvet, with a late-18th-century design, lends its deep green Empire color to the walls and niches, to the sofas and the curtains, and, in fact, sets the tone for the entire room. However, to contrast with this soft harmony, a bold idea was required, to give a sense of excitement. The rug shown here was the answer. Emilio Terry created the lively, rhythmic design of black, white, and lavender-blue triangles which spread out, fan-like, from the center of the room. The rug was made to his design in Portugal.

A rug with originality

GRAND DECORATION
Manors and town houses

Vine-covered walls and a roof of old tiles supported by heavy beams hardly suggest a house decorated in the grand manner of Paris. Yet the style is to be found here with only slight adaptations. These have been made to fit the freer, more informal country setting. The large pieces of furniture are well suited to the fabrics that have been used in profusion throughout the house. In the Louis XIV house at the beginning of the chapter, we see how the 18th-century style takes on a freshness well suited to luxurious country living.

Individual style hardly counts in this ▶ living room; the total effect is what is all important. The special quality of Princess Chavchavadze's decoration is a predilection for understatement. This is apparent, among other things, in her use of fabrics: olive green felt for the shirred hangings on the walls, blond felt with black trim for the table in the foreground, greige velvet for the Louis XVI armchair, and an accenting red for the sofa. The gilt of the picture frames and the bronzes stand out with a subtle brilliance. Each work of art maintains its separate and highly individual identity: the Hubert Robert landscape over the mantelpiece, the 18th-century drawings on the walls, the antique porphyry vase mounted in gilt bronze by Gouthière which shares the table with the 16th-century centaurs, Augsburg caryatids and a large vermeil cachepot.

Tradition is maintained in the dining room, where the table is set for a formal dinner. On the polished 19th-century mahogany surface stand four silver candlesticks, which are ready to be lighted for the meal. The walls are covered with sky-blue Indian silk, and the Régence chairs are in yellow damask. A second painting by Hubert Robert, "The Monuments of Paris," crowns the scene.
▼

Contributing to the charm of this country house near Vézelay (built at the time of Louis XIV) is the attractive mixture of 17th- and 18th-century furniture combined with the wall hangings inspired by the Second Empire. The styles have been cleverly chosen and blended to suit the architectural features of the house. In the main building the decoration was kept simple. Princess Chavchavadze had the interstices of the rough beams covered and painted white so the texture and color would harmonize with the velvets, silks, and other fine materials she planned to use in the room. In the old barn nearby, the beams had to be strengthened with masonry, which gives them their modern look. These beams divide the space, over forty feet long, into four areas. Although the décor is predominantly 18th century and in character with the formal architecture, paradoxically, the impression is of romanticism because of the many odd and charming corners that delight the visitor.

THE 18TH CENTURY IN BURGUNDY
With Second Empire wall hangings

◄ Small ornaments can be very important to the total effect of a room. Here, facing the living room fireplace, is a full-length English portrait dated 1632, and next to it, on the console, a small bronze bust. Both are attractively set off by the green felt walls. The 17th-century furniture, Queen Anne table, and Louis XII armchair are a pleasing combination. Greige felt, flocked with black, was used for the curtains and draperies.

In the barn near the main house, Princess Chav- ► chavadze created a décor in four parts. Against a white background she worked out a warm and delicate palette using cherry red velvet, a Bokhara rug in old rose, a white marble mantelpiece flecked with ivory, and rows of old leather books that line an entire wall. The 18th-century chairs are placed both to suit the irregular architecture and to provide convenient conversation groups.

◄ The smallest room in the house is the front hall. The hanging wall draperies have gray and white stripes that contrast with the light-colored woods of the double-doored Directoire credenza, and the chairs are covered with black horsehair. Notice the unusual placement of the striking horse painting by Alfred de Dreux.

The beams, covered to look almost like vaulting, ► divide the space below into separate areas. This allowed for more than usual diversity in the selection and arrangement of the furniture: the armchair at left is Louis XVI, the chair in the background is Régence, and the one in the foreground is Louis XV. Each piece, whether framed by the buttressed arches or enhanced by the whiteness of the walls, is treated as an ornament.

A corner filled with mementos
adds interest and an intimate feeling.

◀ The appearance of a farmhouse is created by the thatch roof, rough stucco
walls, blue-green shutters, and by the
flowers that surround the house on all
sides behind the low fence.

A country living room expressing rustic
18th-century simplicity. A double door
hidden in the panelling opens onto a
supply of firewood stored for the winter.
▼

A THATCH FARMHOUSE DATED 1960
How to use the odds and ends of the Louis XV period

It is hard to believe that this thatch-roofed house near Rambouillet, with its heavy beams riddled with ancient cracks and its authentic 18th-century panelling, is modern, but in fact the building was completed as recently as 1960. The architect was Victor Ridel of Chantilly, and the contents of the house were chosen by M. and Mme. Henri Dewavrin with the help of Mme. Magliano. Every advantage was taken of modern materials and building techniques. On the ground floor, insulation was achieved by layers of gravel, concrete, and hollow tile laid on its side. Then a second layer of concrete was added before the final flooring. The walls consist of two thicknesses of material with air space between. This would be hard to guess from the exterior with its rough-surface stucco finish. Inside the house the 18th-century panelling also gives no hint of the modern construction. The panelling in the living room comes from a small château of the Louis XV period near Pont-l'Evêque. The beams formerly supported the ceiling of a château near Conches (destroyed in World War II), and the fireplace was brought from a house in Normandy. Even the front hall is paneled with wood taken from a folly near Caen. Although the decorations come from many sources and periods, an extraordinary feeling of unity prevails. Norman panelling, furniture from Provence, modern copies, all blend into a harmonious whole, the intended rustic Louis XV effect being maintained by the patina of natural wood, by the absence of veneer and bronze, and by the stone mantels.

◀ Everything authentic to an old manor house is included in the dining room. The mantelpiece and panelling at one time graced a house at Honfleur, the beams came from an old farmhouse, and the chairs are Provençal. There is a gamut of muted tones: no gilt appears except on the candlesticks, and there are no veneers. Forming an attractive point of interest is the painted tole chandelier mounted with white porcelain flowers.

White walls, painted furniture, and ▶
flowered fabrics contribute to the
lightness and charm of Mme. Dewavrin's bedroom. The screen and the
chest of drawers were decorated
with brightly colored flowers and
birds in the Venetian manner.

The children's dining room also has
an appropriate freshness. The walls
are covered with printed cotton from
the low oak wainscoting to the cornice, and the floor is paved with red
tiles. The furniture is designed to
stand the kind of hard wear that a
child is likely to give it.
▼

The living rooms is predominantly 18th century in feeling, although several styles ▶
have been mixed. The sofas, covered with light willow-green velvet, are modern,
the fireplace was composed from several superb 17th-century relics, the chairs
in front of the Louis XV table are Provençal, and the panelling is Norman.

The tile-paved treads of the staircase, the walls covered with Le Manach chintz,
and the wooden balusters suggest the romantic taste of the past century. The
round clock (which replaced the fashion for bracket clocks), the sloping ceiling
of the landing, and even the beautiful 18th-century doors contribute to the delightful romantic feeling of this front hall.
▼

Flowered fabrics are combined with panelling of the Louis XV period.

The reason for the surprising vigor of the decorations in M. and Mme. Bouchayer's Norman château at Lintot-les-Bois lies partly in the solidity which is common in the buildings in the Dieppe area, partly in the English influence (seen, to begin with, in the 1790 façade), and partly in the way the Louis XVI, Directoire, and English furnishings have been combined in the rooms. There are details of classic authenticity, such as the panelling of the Directoire period in the living room and the Louis XVI armchairs and tables with legs ornamented with stopped fluting. But it is interesting to mention some of the things that one might expect to find in such a setting that are, in fact, missing: the customary accumulation of fragile bibelots, for instance, and the use of fabrics with floral designs. A stern rigor seems to have guided the hand of the decorator, Serge Royaux. On the floors, large areas of subdued, solid-colored, wool carpeting replaces the usual expanses of Savonnerie foliage. The curtains are of solid-colored faille, and the chairs and sofas are covered either with solid fabrics or with embossed velvet of a single hue. When strict adherence to a style is avoided, as here, it is possible to mix many elements and to think largely in terms of comfort : for example, the heavy mass of the large sofas covered in English leather give the house the kind of solid comfort and good taste that Britain enjoyed in the Regency period. The thick pile carpets and the overstuffed leather upholstery, the few low coffee tables and the illumination from the unpretentious table lamps, contribute to the leisurely feeling common to great country houses for which the English are so justly renowned.

LOUIS XVI WITH ENGLISH TOUCHES
A Norman château from the Revolutionary era

On the facing page, superb panelling of the Directoire period, restored by Serge Royaux, sets the tone for the entire room. The sofas and chairs are in the best Louis XVI manner, and the coffee table, which had no forerunner in the 18th century, has been adapted to suit the period. However, there are modern touches. For instance nothing is small or spindly, and although the carpet is placed in the 18th-century manner, it is of solid color and deep pile as opposed to the traditional Savonnerie pattern.

Comfort in good taste,
with thick carpets
and overstuffed
leather chairs

◄ Warm colors relieve the austerity
of the guest room. The daybed in
the alcove and the armchair in
front of the mahogany desk are
in keeping with the style of the old
doors, in which little panes of antique mirror give important touches
of brilliance to the room.

◄ Like the façade of the house, the ►
library is an anglicized version of
French Louis XVI. The wide leather
sofa and the comfortable armchair
might have come straight out of a
London club. The styles blend
without clashing: the glass-fronted
bookcase in the Louis XVI manner,
the desk dating from the Consulat,
and the overstuffed Victorian leather chair near the fireplace.

THE NEW VOGUE FOR WHITE
Without frills or furbelows

It all began with this house — white on the outside and white on the inside. Or rather, the fashion for white began all over again, because the first vogue for predominantly white rooms occurred in 1925. But in this new house in the Ile-de-France, designed by Pierre Barbe, something new has been added. For the first time we see the wedding of white and the eclectic decoration so typical of the last few years, where 18th-century chairs and Victorian sofas become neighbors. Upon entering the large living room, one can at once understand why this house has influenced the new trend despite its rather low ceiling and narrow proportions, for white, not only seems to broaden the space but creates an air of purity and light that is extremely restful. Instead of a cornice, the walls have only a simple molding, and the curtains are hung without valances. In fact, understatement is the watchword. We see it exercised again in the large and comfortable sofa, which, if a strong color instead of white had been used for its covering, would appear too massive for the room. Furthermore, the slip cover has no fringe or tassel. There is also an unusual softness both in the fabric selected for the curtains and in the blue and beige pile rug. Ornaments placed against a white background seem to look ten times as important — for example, the bronze Japanese duck with an olive patina and the dark bronze Chinese hind. Upstairs in the bedroom more Chinese ornaments are to be found — along with more white — which gives a pleasant sense of continuity as one walks through the house. It is perhaps upstairs that the actual key to the charm of the house's whiteness lies. There, under the ceiling that slopes upward to a central beam, a portrait by Matisse and two statues fill the space with their presence. Little else is displayed: a fur throw on the bed, a small Knoll table, and an Oriental rug on the carpeting. But from these few objects and the light-reflecting walls comes an extraordinary atmosphere of comfort and peace. Even though many of the elements are modern, it is not any particular period one thinks of, but the owner's personality as reflected by favorite ornaments placed against the milky white background.

▲
The white walls and the white tub holding the tree echo the white curtains hanging at the entrance to the bedroom. The only bright color is provided by the flooring of brick-red tiles.

◄ **The quality of white changes according to the colors that are placed next to it. The dark, waxed wood of the Régence armchair, the Queen Anne sideboard, and the Louis XIII table make it seem the whitest white. Bright accents (which should. be few against such a light background) make the white seem a little darker. The brass of the Louis XIII candlestick, fitted as a lamp, shines clearly against the white, even from a distance. In the same way, the white of the fine cotton slip cover on the sofa contrasts with the soft hues of the Spanish rug and seems to give it an extra measure of vitality.**

At mealtime the living room becomes a dining room. The splendid 17th-century English table of waxed oak, almost black from years of polishing, is of course the focal point, and the color of the surface is in direct contrast with the white walls and other furnishings. The chairs of waxed wood are early Louis XV, close to Régence, and their caned backs give an appropriate lightness to a room where tapestry and embossed velvet would be out of place.

Classic France meets contemporary England.

Like the canopy of a tent, the white sloping ▶ ceiling of the guest room radiates lightness. All the furniture was chosen for the same evanescent quality: black-and-white English armchairs and white trestle tables, each of light and slender form. Every object displayed here is important, but dominating the entire décor is the Matisse drawing in its thin gilded frame above the bed. The two statues of Chinese peasants catch the eye from a distance, and, at the other end of the room, the bronze bust, set on a trestle table in front of a drawing by Beaurepaire, stands out with greater sharpness than it would if it were placed against a colored background. Under the window, the head by Janine Janet seems to join the Matisse head in watching over the scene.

The pure geometry of the black metal staircase, with its red tiles, finds a perfect background in the clear white walls.
▼

FUNDAMENTALS OF THE "HAUTE EPOQUE"

A manor house in the Ile-de-France

▲
Backed by the ancient park, the house at Pré Saint-Jean replaced the razed château. The white limestone and the glazed tiles are now all that remind us of the older building.

Green, red, and brown are the ▶ typical colors of the "Haute Epoque" palette. But the red here has a touch of fallow, like the terra cotta of the tiles and the polished leather on the chairs. The green has a touch of blue, as in this Enghien tapestry, and the brown encompasses all the variations of old wood in this library which is set aside for the works of the owner's father, Baron Ernest Seillière.

In several ways Pré Saint-Jean, in the Ile-de-France countryside near Senlis, is a perfect illustration of the major trend of decoration in the past five years which dispenses with many established and preconceived notions. For Baron and Baroness Seillière, Pré Saint-Jean was rich in memories and mementos, but all that remained of the great 1880 house was an empty shell surrounded by the fine park. Raymond Busse, their architect, leveled the old structure and built a new house that was much smaller, yet maintained the generous scale of the older one. The owners wanted no decorating for the sake of decorating; they wanted straightforward and honest materials — such as natural wood for the banisters and for the panelling in the dining room, bare white walls devoid of all molding or ornamentation and plain terra-cotta tiles for flooring. The first requirement in the over-all plan was to leave each material in its natural state, to be in the spirit of the "Haute Epoque." The second requirement was to organize the space of the rooms adroitly and asymmetrically (only the dining room, where a French window opens on to the garden and forms a central axis, was an exception made). The third requirement, to avoid clutter, was to use no tiny ornaments and not to allow any picky details — the rule not necessarily applying to scale as much as to proportion and quality. As a result, everything in the house has a powerful and monumental look, right down to the smallest box of Limousin champlevé enamel. The fourth requirement (and perhaps the most important one) was to use antique colors only. These are all muted, ranging from brick to old blackened oak, from chair leather to the faded hues of Oriental rugs. All that remained to do after following these planned requirements was to position the heavy 16th- and 17th-century furniture, with its strong and forceful shapes. The owners' collection of ornaments brings a very personal quality to the décor. A strong bond is established between the Gothic reliquary, the Chinese Kiun Yao of the Sung dynasty, the medieval wrought-iron candlestick, and the peasant basin that came from Alsace. This only happens with objects that have authority, regardless of their period, size, or place of origin.

▲

In the dining **room**, the surface of the table is inlaid with fragments of antique **Dutch** tiles which establish the color scheme. The pine panelling around a Flemish tapestry in autumn-leaf tones is finished to match the old timbers that frame the table.

◀ The semicircular bookshelves solve two problems. Since bookcases were unknown at this period, these built-in shelves of old wood are a good substitute, and they make a fine display case for the rich leather bindings. The semicircular shape softens the rather severe feeling of the decoration and also makes a perfect background for the large, round library table that dominates the room.

In the front hall, the floor and treads of the staircase are set with antique tile which is held in place with strips of wood. In the living room, the mantelpiece (made from a beam set on two Gothic supports), the tile flooring, and the Henri II furniture are all in perfect harmony. Arranged to one side of the room are four chairs and a square gaming table. The sketch on the wall has an interesting history: it is a design by the painter **Le Rosso** for the great hall at **Fontainebleau**.

The undisguised power of "Haute Epoque"

◄ The sense of Gothic height is contradicted in the master bedroom. The palette and the details as well evoke the interiors of a Pieter de Hooch. The floor is paved with old Flemish glazed tiles. The wainscoting and the shutters were extracted from the backs of old church pews. The bed is surmounted by a canopy and placed according to medieval custom. Two Henry II armchairs, and a glazed vase holding a lily worthy of Durer complete a composition that owes a lot to the old masters.

Flying horizontal lines guided the decorating scheme of the studio. Not a single high piece of furniture was allowed in. The entire plan is based on the geometry of the complex space that sets the radiating spokes of the beams against the chessboard of the flooring. Even the mantel, which is made of a fine sculptured Norman beam of the 16th century, is constructed to accentuate the horizontal feeling. The low, stumpy chairs seem made to measure for a décor that appears to be compressed by a hidden force.

▼

The palette of Dutch primitives.

THE HÔTEL DE CORNOUAILLES AT SENLIS
The aura of the age of Henri IV

This old town house can be found on the rue du Chat-Haret in the midst of other Renaissance houses, north of the cathedral. Indoors, a recent and very successful restoration job has uncovered the original 16th-century character of the rooms. In the main living room, where the walls had been plastered over, the beautiful stone of Senlis has been revealed, and its color, a reddish tan, looks extremely well with the oak beams. To keep the furniture as much as possible in character with the age of the building, Mr. Yassukovich, an American who fell in love with Senlis, patiently collected oak pieces of the 17th century. Most of this furniture is as cracked with age as the timbers. The decorator of the house, Mrs. Dolly Hoffmann, selected Oriental rugs in varied but quiet colors that harmonize with the oak flooring. In the dining room, which is essentially 18th century, there are traces of other periods, mostly played down in the interests of maintaining unified effect. The beams are uncovered but are painted to match the panelling on the walls. Undoubtedly the modern love for materials and textures influenced Mrs. Hoffmann in the way she has contrasted wrinkled stone with tapestries, and old tiles (uncovered in a bedroom under the flooring) with Oriental rugs of luxurious wool. Everything was planned with the utmost care, and each separate but related plan has been scrupulously respected, as is mandatory in all large-scale decoration. For instance, the positions of all the Oriental rugs follow the transverse pattern of the main ceiling beams. However, a few liberties have been taken with tradition, and all the furniture is not of the same period. Thus we see a Louis XV desk standing cater-cornered in the fashion that dates from the 18th century, and a sofa (facing the fireplace) backed by a long Louis XIII table in the fashion imported from Georgian England. The principal rule followed in the arrangement and choice of the furniture was the avoidance of anything that lacked character. A set of Delft vases could very well stand next to a Renaissance tapestry provided it harmonized in shape, color, and material; in other words, an 18th-century ornament was a suitable choice, provided that it had quality and was in proper scale and harmony with the room.

▲
The dignity of the end of the 16th century marks the façade of this old Henri IV town house and was the sole inspiration for the décor.

◀ The "uncovered" look that the owner chose to feature does more honor to the old house than a museum-like restoration would have done. The walls of naked stone harmonize superbly with the subtle shades of the polished natural wood of the Louis XIII armchairs and the table with the diamond pattern. They also complement well the restrained colors of the tapestry and the Oriental rugs.

When Louis XV and
Louis XIII are neighbors

▲
Even 18th-century interior design can be vigorous. It is a matter of proportion, colors, and the selection of objects. Here, the generous size of the Régence furniture gives great strength to the room. The chairs, painted green and cream, harmonize with the white beams and panelling and even seem to become part of the architecture.

◄ The carefully calculated contrast of straightforward, almost rough, materials with touches of more sophisticated fabrics and woods gives a subtle and intimate feeling that admirably suits this bedroom in the 17th-century manner. The original tile floor, discovered under a later wood floor, the Persian rug, the mirror with a Louis XIII gilt wood frame, and the embossed jute on the walls are played off against one another most ingeniously.

THE BLENDING OF PAST AND PRESENT

A house by architect Pierre Barbe

▲
The atmosphere of older estates has been ingeniously suggested by architect Pierre Barbe. The proportions are those that are typical of the 18th-century follies built at the gates of Paris. The front door with its faintly arched frame accentuates this feeling of an older era.

A fresco of antique glazed tiles decorates the completely ▶ modern kitchen. Pierre Barbe chose the zoning principle that originated in the United States, but he has used traditional materials : yellow ocher ceramic tile for the work counter and the splashboard, wood with wrought-iron hardware for the cabinets. The carved wooden chairs are in the Baroque tradition, and they—like the frescoes—pay witty homage to the past. The same lightheartedness is apparent in the pantry, where other Spanish tiles are the main decoration. In mock solemnity they watch over the lavabo.

This house at Marnes-la-Coquette, designed by Pierre Barbe, proves that classical styles are still valid. It also demonstrates that it is effective, occasionally, to introduce elements that break with tradition. There were an inadequate garage and a tiny cottage for a caretaker on this property that had been in the family since the end of the last century. Pierre Barbe kept only the foundations, on which he built an 18th-century folly. But here and there he integrated modern features, such as the new garage, that make it look as if there had been additions to the house through the years. The owners followed the same principle inside the house. In the dining room, the vaulting is modern, the mantelpiece evokes the Renaissance, and the linen-fold panelling on the door strikes a medieval note. Adjoining is the living room with white walls against which a black, overstuffed, and very Victorian-looking sofa is placed as the focal point. The mixture continues both in the kitchen, where, in the midst of a modern zoned plan, carved wooden chairs of Spanish design are used, and in the bathroom, where the fixtures are modern but the murals are painted in the manner of old prints. Upstairs there is an attic remodeled as a study, where cabinets of red pine serve as a background for a few modern paintings. Here, through the narrow dormer windows, one can enjoy the view of a half-Renaissance, half-English garden that bears the contemporary mark of landscape designer Russell Page.

As in many old attics, things just seem to accumulate in this room, which was planned as a study. Pierre Barbe has avoided symmetry and given the whole area an improvised look. Cabinets of red pine serve as a display stand for ship models. The furniture is of the kind that, years ago, was usually relegated to the attic—an English desk, for instance, and Thonet rocking chairs. On the wall, which is covered with saffron velvet, hangs a gilt-framed 19th-century portrait.

The staircase with open risers follows the tradition ▶ of attic stairs. It gives access to the shelves of books that line the walls, and it leads up to a studio. Mixed in with the books are ornaments that remind one of the great voyages of former times, from the little gouache of a man-of-war in its Louis Philippe frame to the fossil fish.

Brand new
architecture evokes
the memories
of bygone centuries.

▲
The dining room, which is vast enough to resemble the front halls of olden times, doubles here as the entrance to the house. Narrow vaults, painted white, give a rhythmic quality to the ceiling. The mixture of furnishings is midway between "Haute Epoque" and rustic: a mantelpiece in the medieval tradition, two doors with linen-fold panelling brought back from Spain, primitive paintings also from Spain, and a table and chairs that are Spanish Louis XV. The stairs at the right lead down to a powder room, billiard room, heater room, and laundry. The modern openwork gate at the top of the stairs — an idea borrowed from American architecture — is in curious contrast with some of the nearby antique details. In the living room, Pierre Barbe has used the same ingenious counterpoint of old and new.

The furniture is Victorian and the architecture is quite modern. The huge ▶ overstuffed sofa covered in black watered silk is as romantic in its own way as the primitive Spanish paintings that hang above it. Everything seems entirely at home under the shallow, rounded vaults. And with the Louis XIV goblets hung from the ceiling like a mobile, the fusion of past and present is satisfactorily complete.

A HUNTING LODGE AT YPRES

the return to an older tradition: the flemish version

▲

The Flemish landscape of fields and calm waters sets the theme of simple hospitality and the robust decoration of another age. From the front hall to the attic, the decoration owes its unity to the effect of unpainted wood against a background of white walls. Under the rafters, the dormitory for the young hunters has the martial simplicity that suits the sport (below right).

In the front hall, the only decoration is a long gunrack that stands ▶ on an oak sideboard enhanced by molding. Everything else is restrained to give full play to the solid charm of the ceiling beams and the brick-red checkerboard of the floor tiles.

At a turning in the hall, a small wooden table punctuates the décor. There is no particular period and no affectation here, nothing, in fact but the play of materials and archaic lines that is worthy of an interior by Holbein.

▼

Was it the picture of Belgium, with its bright green fields bordering calm waterways, that imperceptibly influenced the decoration that M. and Mme. Steverlynck chose for their house at Ypres? They intended to use this house, designed by Pierre Barbe in the tradition of the Bruges alms-houses, as a hunting lodge, and so the rough, robust vigor of the "Haute Epoque" seemed an ideal solution. When one thinks of hunting, trophies such as skins and mounted heads come to mind rather than the exquisitely fragile designs of the 18th century. For this reason, the owners decided that, under the powerful beams of blackened oak, it would be suitable to use the heavy, chunky forms of Italian and Renaissance tables, and also to introduce smaller tables with turned legs that were common in most European countries in the 17th century. But at the same time they wanted their house to express the idea of cheerful vacation evenings. Consequently, they added furniture of simple design and of recent manufacture. They also favored wrought iron, wood, stone, brick, and other "earthy" materials such as pottery, but rigorously avoided anything that might appear too austere or gloomy. The Flemish sense of color inspired the floor of the dining room, with its black flagstones from Tournai set off by a network of tiles from Boom. The seat cushions are in an olive green borrowed from the palette of Vermeer. The appreciation of comfort, so typical of the Low Countries, inspired the deep sofas designed for pleasant evenings in front of the fire. Everything is massive and vigorous, in the spirit of the period that was chosen. Superfluous ornament is avoided. Against the white walls, the design of the flagging, the large area of glowing velvet on the sofas, the bright accent of the yellow chair cushions in the dining room, give this 17th-century decoration the strong colors of a Flemish festival.

Wood, stone and brick; the aroma of the soil.

▲
This completely Mediterranean dining room mixes an Italian table with Spanish chairs. The oak door takes its inspiration from the hue and panelling of the 17th-century armoire. The floor has black flagstones from Tournai framed four by four with tiles from Boom. Upholstered chairs would be perhaps out of place next to a Renaissance table, but these Spanish chairs are as rigid as Gothic spires, and the seat cushions provide unexpectedly soft notes.

Comfort can be made to look austere and keep the spirit of the ▶ Renaissance as long as certain harmonies of mass, of line and of color are respected. Nothing is more genial than deep sofas and armchairs set before the living room hearth. These have the massive, monumental charm that goes with robust decoration. From the modern coffee table solidly planted on the floor and the little end table of blackened oak buttressed by splayed legs to the completely modern raised hearth and the Henry IV table that backs up to the sofa, everything seems thrust to the floor by the same force that raises the beams in this perfect living room for autumn evenings.

◀ **To the left of the fireplace a door leads to a bar under the eaves where guests who are beer-lovers — often the case in Flanders — can fill their glasses. A refrigerating unit installed between the barrels and the pump keeps the beer at the right temperature.**

KEYS TO DECORATING

The personal touch

What can be done with a very classical, plain interior? Pilasters of carved wood and delicate moldings supply the right architectural background. A collection of porcelain birds on brackets gives the room an original theme. A china chandelier and a monkey's cage provide the focal point that is lacking. In short, anything can be done, as seen in this dining room belonging to the **Duc de Talleyrand**, if one has decorating keys such as those described on the following pages.

Here is a triumph of objets d'art on a wall where paintings are massed and on tables where small boxes line up in rows. But this is a far cry from simple accumulation. For his **Bérard** drawings, his **Cocteau** designs for "The Infernal Machine" and for his portrait of the writer as a child, **Boris Kochno** chose an expert layout. The rhythm of the paintings carries over to the étagère and even echoes the planes and angles of the furniture. With his boxes he alternated gold with other materials. Many are the work of **Fabergé**, among them the snuffbox surmounted with a Negro's head carved in semi-precious sapphire matrix. Just inches away is a "**Box for Cigarette Butts**", a present from **Picasso** in 1943. This illustrates the first important principle of an object as part of a decorating scheme : avoid at all costs the kind of series of similar examples one finds in museums. The second principle: pay great attention to the background and don't just spread a collection out anywhere. Here the dark wood of a radiophonograph highlights the brilliant yellow of the gold and the delicate shadings of the tortoise shell.

COLLECTIONS KNOW NO BOUNDS

They have jumped off the table onto the walls.

▲

In this 18th-century room, a collection of Dresden and Sèvres porcelain has a subtle effect on the entire decoration. The panelling has a simple molding and is painted in a single, pale shade that creates a restful background. The embroidered silk on the Louis XV sofa and chairs is in a floral pattern that is repeated by the porcelain on the small Louis XV and Louis XVI tables that stand around the room. The objects on each of these tables are displayed symmetrically, and they strike a sparkling note in every corner of the otherwise conventional room.

The harmony of bronze and marble inspired these two ▶ displays by M. and Mme. Delbée. For the center of both tables — one of them Directoire, the other Second Empire — a converted antique oil lamp was chosen. Each display has its theme. The first one is historic, with heads of Roman emperors and leading figures of Napoleon's day. The other represents the animal kingdom and includes a pair of elephant candlesticks, camels on chased bases, and gilt bronze lions. Objects that previously were merely part of a collection — a French 18th-century dog, an ivory greyhound's head that was a cane handle, a duck's head — now take on the added dimension of being the center of interest in the decoration of the room.

Tabletop decoration:
everything is miniature in scale

The collector's room: its walls become lighted vitrines

(above opposite, left to right)

Foliage and garlands as a motif are used here to blend a collection of blue Sevres, Saxe and Chinese export to the Louis XIV wainscoting. Henri Samuel has stretched velvet over niches that look like jewel boxes.

An opening in the wall between two rooms was purposely preserved, and a vitrine made entirely of glass lets one see the collection from either side. The lighting along the top and the sides is shadowless but never blinding.

Engraved glasses and crystal are seen at their best when placed in front of a picture window. Every hour of the day shows them in a different light. The glass shelves are mounted on tension poles, so that the installation is not permanently fixed and can be changed to suit the owner's whim.

◀ **Like a show window, the panelling of a man's office opens up to hold a collection of ancient arms, arbalests, daggers and hunting horns. Pierre Barbe chose a bronze-green velvet to set off the composition, to enhance the patina of the old ivory and to soften the possible severe notes of the steel.**

Like a classic wainscoting, display cases line all ▶ **four walls of the small sitting room that Pierre Balmain remodeled to hold his famous collection, one of the most complete of the work of Gallé: vases, cups and jars, all first-class examples of the creations of his different periods.**

A small gallery in the Directoire manner was designed by Emilio Terry to house the Greek vases and marbles collected by M. and Mme. Stavros Niarchos. For a collection of this stature, a rather formal room was necessary. This was accomplished with ebony columns topped by gilded capitals and standing on mahogany bases, and with a cornice and doors that are also mahogany, ebony, and gilt bronze. Set against a background of green fabric bordered with a Greek key design, these objects in the Niarchoses' Hôtel de Chanaleilles have true classic dignity. There is no glass, no protection; nothing comes between the beautiful objects and the eye of the beholder.

In the house of decorator Jean Dive, subtle but bizarre ideas ▶ abound, as in his entrance hall where carved coconuts stand in serried rows amid a collection of treen.

Fine ivories by Grollier de Servière (1593-1686) and his disciples ▶ ▶ are displayed by themselves in Mme. Delbée's house. Each piece has its own bracket in the alcove. The indirect lighting is planned so that the ivories are not exposed to undue heat.

Objects displayed where collectors can touch as well as see them

▲
In this room by decorator Serge Royaux, the arangement of
the pictures, which resembles a wall of panelling, is the major
decorative element. A collection of drawings by Helleu, Boldini,
Raffet, and Forain hangs at the head of a mahogany bed by
Georges Jacob. Almost all the drawings have dark mats and
slim, gilded frames, so that they stand out against the solid
color of the wall.

◄ Paintings dominate this room designed by M. Costi, a sculptor
who was for many years the colleague of decorator Emilio Terry.
In the center of the wall is a "Lucrece Stabbing Herself" of the
school of Fontainebleau, which is matched in the small bronze
copy of the "Medici Venus" that stands on top of the Louis XVI
rolltop desk. The three rows of paintings follow the same
vertical lines as the Venus and the two green obelisks.

Pierre Balmain made this collection of 19th-century prints, ▶
drawings, and paintings for his staircase wall. Massed in this
way, they have much greater impact than they would if the
had been spread out. The wall has the charm of a family album,
except that here each item is a little masterpiece.

The decorative use of natural objects

◀ A collection of minerals surrounds the table, and one piece was framed to hang on the wall above the lamp. The colors of the agates and amethysts stand out as beautifully against the carpeting as though it were the velvet lining of a display cabinet. This unusual idea is by designer Philippe Barbier.

In the same house, other minerals ▶ are displayed in cabinets built into the panelling. Crossed steel rods support examples of fluorite, apophyllite, and two quartzes.

Here minerals decorate the cabinet ▶ ▶ doors. Fossil ammonites stand out against panels of raw linen framed by graceful molding.

By their very nature, coral and Gorgonia, necks of amphorae, and whale vertebrae supply an unexpected decorative note, and Michel Pignères—a snorkeling buff—has used a handsome mahogany vitrine to display them to maximum advantage. (Above right.)

Small shells are decoratively arranged on the shelves of a Napoleon III mahogany étagère, where they remind the owner of many romantic summer journeys.

Olivier Mourgue pays tribute to the ▶ ▶ egg by displaying his collection in shadow boxes on the bookshelf.

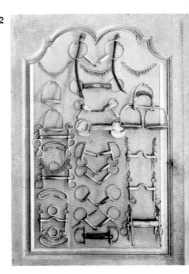

Unusual collections
that repeat the same theme
over and over again for effect.

5

7

6

8

1 Scrimshaw can occupy an important place in decoration. Here antique collector Maurice Génis has placed carvings by 18th- and 19th-century sailors on a simple table and also on black brackets set against an olive gray wall.

2 A montage of bits, stirrups, and curb chains replaces the usual floral carving on this panelling. The objects reflect decorator André Mercier's interest in hunting, a sport he enjoys at Berengeville-la-Campagne.

3 Time stands still. A collection of 19th-century copper clock pendulums decorates a wall in M. and Mme. Louis Sorrel-Dejerine's apartment.

4 Instead of being arranged on a table in the customary way, this collection of treenwas mounted on wall brackets, where it makes an interesting pattern against the light-colored, waxed pine panelling.

5 Marble and bronze columns and obelisks are lined up in a rhythmic pattern of cylinders and pyramids. Small ornaments take on added importance when they are massed together in this way.

6 Grotesque 19th-century candlesticks arranged on a table by decorator Jean Dive. The group has the comic air of a troupe on parade.

7 An ordinary wall suddenly takes on an entirely new aspect when covered with rows of old keys. Here they seem to float as if in a dream, and guests can only ponder on the meaning — if any — of the symbolism.

8 Streaked round globes of Italian marble provide an air of fantasy in this corner of Pierre Balmain's house. The solidity of the balls contrasts with the delicate stands of turned wood, each one of different height.

▲
A four-thousand-year-old marble statue from the Cyclades, despite its modest size, dominates this room. Face lifted, arms crossed, it watches over the scene. Only an object with a clear-cut shape, such as the simple dish that stands near it, is an appropriate accompaniment.

▲
The decorator Dominique Mailliard has brought together a unique trio — an Agni leopard from the Ivory Coast, a seated pre-Columbian figure from Mexico, and paintings by Miró — to express the power of primal forces. In a room where the decorating has been stripped to essentials, these elements combine to create a feeling of tension and excitement.

◄ A collection of Peruvian pottery makes a fascinating corner decoration. The walls are white so as show to full advantage the soft brick and ivory colors painted on the pots. The arrangement of the little shelves has been ingeniously staggered to avoid too rigid a look.

Primitive objects: the force of unsophisticated art

In the calm atmosphere of a hall decorated in the 18th-century style, a painting by **Sonia Delaunay** seems to slide quietly into place against the gray walls, and suddenly gives the room an entirely new dimension. The sofa is Régence, and the bronze by James Brower.

◄ Here the alcove is decorated with panelling painted to resemble real wood. The daybed is upholstered in beige-gold velvet, and over it hangs a large abstract painting by Soulages. On the coffee table is a sculpture by Arman, made entirely of forks massed together.

Between two 18th-century windows, Roger Vivier has hung a Poliakoff dating from 1953. The 16th-century Spanish frame makes it possible to mix abstract art with furniture from the ancien régime. ▼

DECORATING WITH MODERN ART

Unsuspected affinities
with the 18th-century.

The waves of watered silk bring their dancing rhythm to the paintings of Poliakoff and Fautrier, of Max Ernst and Bernard Buffet. They flow down the walls and right over the sofa to blend modern art and traditional furniture into a single theme, unified by the green of the walls and floor, in the manner dear to the decorateur Serge Royaux.

Painting can bridge the gap between antique and modern furnishings.

▲
Like a huge fresco, a painting by Kijno spreads dominant blues and whites over the gray wall. Roger Vivier's decoration has clear-cut lines with solid colors and classic furniture in leather upholstery.

In the foreground is a white marble sculpture by Signori on top of a Gothic column, and in the background is an angular abstraction by Atlan dated 1935. This painting was framed by Roger Vivier in wrought iron to give it the same solidity as the sculpture. Below the painting are two Louis XVI chairs and a marble-topped console table.

◄◄ Panelling is always an attractive background for pictures. Here "The Olive Trees," a painting by Vieira da Silva, hangs over two drawings by H. Laurens. The bronze on the table is also by Laurens.

◄ "The Metamorphoses of Proteus" by Labisse has the rigid quality of bronze in this mantelpiece arrangement by Marie-Laure de Noailles. On the mantel itself she has arranged a handsome row of Renaissance bronzes.

"Encre de Chine 1960," a striking ► work by Alechinsky, goes admirably with the collection of primitive objects that decorator Henri Samuel (of the firm of Alavoine) has collected for his own house.

To blind these huge blinding windows, Serge Royaux hung them with raw silk curtains and then softened the light with the help of dyed scrim. He has topped off this wall and the others with the same valance to recreate the architectural feeling that was lacking.

A wall of curtains in finely striped caramel velvet echoes the wall covering in this Paris living-room of Mme Bory. An ingenious system makes it possible to pull them closed so that the folds are straight, to push them completely to one side or divide them into three sections as you see them here.

To create wall space for his furniture, the owner of this apartment reduced the excessive window area with a fixed six-foot section of fabric that seems to prolong the green-almond corduroy curtains on each side. Against this panel hangs an Audubon print.

For French doors, straight-hung curtains; and for ▶ the center area (divided into a double-size window and two sliding doors opening onto a balcony), wide seaweed-green curtains with tiebacks. Victor Grand-pierre unifies it all in this room of the Marquis de La Falaise by using box pleats on all the curtains and a round curtain rod of black iron for the entire wall.

Curtains in triple depth, with the under-curtains of teal ▶ ▶ blue and diaphanous glass curtains allowed Jean Dessès to minimize the width of an outsize window.

CURTAINS AND DRAPERIES

Large glass areas in modern apartments acquire a new look.

◄ The problem of hanging curtains on sloping walls was solved here by the use of tiebacks and simple box pleats instead of valances. The major remodeling of the Duc and Duchesse d'Harcourt's apartment was planned by Pierre Barbe.

▲
Let into the ceiling, the sheer curtains and draperies, which hang the full height of the room, seem to be an extension of the fabric-covered walls. This is an admirable plan for a small room where a more conventional treatment would be overpowering. The quiet decoration by Androuchka strikes exactly the right note for the home of an author.

◄ Green and white cretonne curtains, hung at cornice height, help to keep the window in scale with the rest of the room at the Château de Baillon. Mme. Bemberg used the same garlanded fabric for the curtains, the walls, and the sofa, to give unity and a romantic air to the entire room.

Hung behind the panelling, swagged curtains repeat the curved ► lines of the window openings. The panelling for this handsome room belonging to M. and Mme. Jacques Abreu was found in Normandy by Henri Samuel of the firm of Alavoine.

Curtains must follow the curves of the panelling,
adjust to the height of the ceiling, and sometimes
hang from sloping walls.

Portières establish a dividing line.

The draperies of this hall draw back to reveal a 19th-century plaster cast that used to stand in a garden. Androuchka has used portières to create a series of such vistas in this apartment, which belongs to a distinguished author.

A single portière delimits the two parts of this living room but does not make two separate rooms. The placement of the furniture also suggests a dividing line. (Below left.)

Draperies are used to give importance to the living room entrance. The handsome fabric, in muted stripes of green, old rose, and pale beige, is sufficiently impressive without any valance or braid.

Although these olive-green por- ► tières are high and wide, they are in scale with the rest of the room in Raymond Alexandre's residence. So is the mahogany table. The decorator was Gérard Mille.

Simple and sumptuous, a single portière of garnet velvet (which matches the curtains) separates Jean Dessès's dining room from his adjoining smoking room. Victor Grandpierre was the decorator.

A portière of banana-yellow faille, asymmetric like the architecture of this hall, reveals the staircase leading to the upper floors. The tassels, fringe, and complex swagging are typically Napoleon III.
▼

CONVERSATION GROUPS

Even though each essential element serves a practical purpose, it takes a skillful eye to arrange an attractive conversation group.

A conversation group in one corner of the living-room is modern in feeling. Facing an angled sofa covered in green velvet are two Barcelona chairs by Mies van der Rohe. Yves Saint Laurent, the owner, has put a Chinese bronze goose on the table as a major ornament.

The grouping around the fireplace in Mme. Jean Ralli's house is in the English manner. Victor Grandpierre, the decorator, has used lettuce green velvet on the sofas and chintz on the two large armchairs. The mantel is a fine example of the Transition period.

An alcove can be used for an intimate conversation ▶ group, as Victor Grandpierre shows in his placing of the sofa. This is covered in an old-gold-colored velvet. Completing the group are two Blanchard armchairs in blue velvet and a bergère in tones of red and gold.

▲
A fireplace and two love seats make a small conversation corner for evening entertaining and têtes-à-têtes. The soft green velvet, the caramel-colored walls, and the milky whiteness of the antique Empire mantelpiece provide a quiet and restful background. The girandole mirror stands out as the focal point of the entire arrangement.

Grouped in front of a wide window overlooking the Invalides are over- ▶ stuffed armchairs of Napoleon III vintage, a sofa covered in silk leopard pile, and a black lacquer coffee table designed by Gérard Mille. Since this is the principal group in the room, it occupies the main space and faces the view. The apartment belongs to M. and Mme. Bory.

Multiple groupings in large living rooms

An English look distinguishes this living room at the British Embassy in Paris. Lady Gladwyn has used her own mementos and personal possessions. The mantel is Directoire, the furniture is Regency, and the idea of placing the furniture in a conversation group so that it faces the fireplace is Georgian.

◄ In this 18th-century setting with Louis XVI panelling and classic porportions, the usual rule of grouping chairs around small tables has not been followed. M. de Pindray has broken even further with tradition by using a shaggy monochrome rug, a coffee table covered with white Formica, and two contrasting sofas, one Louis XIII and the other modern.

Jacques Regnault wanted the living room in this Flem- ► ish country house to be comfortable, and the deep, wide, soft armchairs and sofas set the pace for the décor. The open-arm chairs are covered in tobacco-brown leather. Sky-blue chintz was used on the other armchairs and the sofa, while the carpet (by Jansen) is a deep green.

Conversation groups
in the middle of the room

The **Coromandel lacquer work that** ▶
fascinated the 18th century sup-
plies a note of brilliance to a subdued décor. Here decorator Gérard
Mille has used a 12-panel screen to
make a Louis XV room seem larger than it is.

A mahogany grille, well suited to
the Regency furniture, was used
by Andrée Higgins to separate a
dining-room from a hall without
losing a pleasant open feeling.
▼

◀ The screen by Vuillard in M. and
Mme. Jacques Abreu's living-room
shows the Place Vintimille as the
painter saw it from his studio
window. The Savonnerie rug and
the embossed velvet upholstery
pick up the same vivid colors.

The scenic wallpaper entitled ▶
"Street Scene in Newport" used
on this screen goes perfectly with
the English feeling of the room.
The screen stands in one corner
of a room that doubles as a studio
and hides an easel and other
painting equipment.

THE RETURN OF THE SCREEN

A screen can set the tone for an entire decorative
scheme, yet still have
all the charm of a delightful improvisation.

▲
A screen of painted **Cordovan** leather dominates the decoration of Jean Dessès's living room. It looks well next to a fine painting by **Suzanne Valadon** in which the same reds and yellows are featured. The bold design of the **Aubusson** rug provides a perfect counterfoil for the screen.

The effective use of screens with plain walls

The dining room in the Hotel **Séguier** was inspired by an Empire watercolor. ▶
First, decorator **Serge Royaux** had the panelling painted to resemble the grain of pine. In two corners of the room he put mahogany screens hung with panels of bronze-green taffeta. Then he added a dozen Louis XVI armchairs (signed by **Lelarge**) that are crisply upholstered in black morocco.

FLOORING

Marble, parquet,
or tile?

▲
Parquet finished in black was used in the dining room of the
Marquis and Marquise de La Falaise. Victor Grandpierre used
a black herringbone pattern to offset the gold raw silk curtains
and the shining silver vases on the two mahogany étagères.
The vases are filled with roses.

◄ Black marble squares (1) are enhanced by white borders and a
gray background. The traditional white flooring decorated
with black plugs (2) can be replaced with polychrome marbles (3) in blue, green, red, and black set in a stone background. An English parquet floor (4) can have strips of teak
separating mahogany planks. Convex tiling (5) is the most
recently revived of the classic flooring materials.

Strips of waxed oak frame the terra-cotta tiles in a front hall ►
that doubles as a living area. Formal and informal furnishings
were chosen by decorator Fred de Cabrol for the Château de
La Roche d'Iré. The handsome provincial Directoire chest
and the blue India print curtains (held in place by tiebacks)
help to emphasize a feeling that is half farmhouse, half château.

THE LOOK WE GIVE OUR ROOMS

How to arrange the furniture.

From the front door to the terrace, a house can take on as many different aspects as it has rooms, even when the style and degree of formality remain the same. But front halls and living rooms must obey certain rules that are quite different from those which apply to bedrooms and dining rooms. If you line the furniture up against the wall in a living room, it may perhaps look solemn and rigid. But line it up in a front hall, as Mrs. Haseltine did in her Paris house, and the result is a charming, countrified look that is entirely suitable for a home that used to be a posthouse when Auteuil was a country village.

At the foot of the stairs

From classic pomp to rustic simplicity the principle is the same : to give rhythm to the perspectives that begin and end at the bottom step.

FRONT HALLS

◀ In the Château d'Houville, built in the 17th century and remodeled under Louis XV, a carpet based on an antique design emphasizes the flowing rhythm of the steps. A painted metal urn filled with hydrangeas and ivy looks gay and welcoming against the staircase and helps to soften the transition from stair to hall. The walls are covered in a yellow-green fabric specially woven at Lyons for the Baronne de Nervo on the advice of Mme. de Grandsaignes. The engravings, a still life, and an antique mirror attract the eye upwards.

For a house in the mountains, the country look is imme- ▶ diately established by the red tile floor, with each tile crisply outlined in white mortar. An antique churn converted into an umbrella stand also emphasizes the rustic quality. On the wall, a saint of polychrome wood watches over the scene near a gleaming copper lavabo.

In the style of...

The 17th and 18th centuries: variations on two themes

ENTRANCES

▲
This is classic decoration brought up to date, with no alterations in the original style of the architecture. The stone and slate floor and the imposing door frames in hallway of the Hôtel Séguier date from the era of the Louis XIV, but the new color harmonies make a great difference. Serge Royaux, the decorator, used a heavy blue fabric with embossed stripes for the walls. He covered the banquettes in the same fabric, and by decorating them with black braid, he made it possible to use the modern banquettes in a basically classic room. Similarly, the huge blue wall areas make a perfect background for the primitive paintings by Desnos, framed in white molding to match the woodwork. Accenting the setting are two white-lacquered arm-chairs upholstered in black leather. These were de-
◄ signed by Georges Jacob.

A dash of romanticism can result in a charming parody ►
of the 17th-century style. A medieval geometry that is typical of the style is apparent in the tile floor, which is the color of toast. Handsome sconces of copper and ebony evoke memories of torches on the walls of old castles. The fresh, bright décor of this front hall is reminiscent of Flemish farmhouses.

ENTRANCES

Wit and fantasy

The fashion for surrealism came late to decoration. There are no rules to this game, except that of giving free rein to the imagination.

◄ A touch of surrealism is introduced here in homage to Salvador Dali, but the fine collection of medallions above the umbrella stand is more in keeping with the classic entrance.

◄ A cat in an obelisk that serves as a display case for a collection of white pottery parodies the marbles, porcelains, and general pomp of the 18th century. The Spanish wool rug has a bright blue inset surrounded by bold scrollwork—a vigorous design that ignores the traditions of the 18th century.

▲
On a real cotton rug, a fake leopard drawn by Fornassetti lies in front of a chest-on-chest covered with an array of trompe l'œil pistols, keys, and parchments. Real canvas creates a tentlike effect overhead. This witty semi-classic front hall is by Ribouldingue and Filochard.

Painted tole monkeys keep watch on either side of a large ►
mirror with an etched-glass frame. The bust of the young man on the reproduction Louis XVI console seems to be smiling at the scene, while the fine 18th-century Turkish rug joins in this quiet mockery of ''great art.''

BEDROOMS

Canopy beds

They are the essence of femininity, whether lavishly formal or in fresh country style.

▲

A baldaquin was the perfect choice for this romantic adaptation of the 18th century. Here the shantung canopy and side curtains match the curtains at the window and stand out against the strong background of embossed turquoise velvet. In fact, the whole decoration in this room is planned around the play of fabrics: wall-to-wall carpeting with a figured rug under the bed, and, on the table, a floral Genoese velvet.

◄ Classic, 18th-century decoration inspired the design of this bed. The same rose and silver figured silk was used to cover the canopy, the bed, the Louis XVI step stool, and the Louis XV chairs. This typically 18th-century practice requires a panelled room and fine furniture. The small table at the foot of the bed is by Carlin, and the secretary is by Schey. The two Chinese vases have Louis XVI mounts.

A charming India print gives an informal air to this 18th-century-style canopy that shelters a Louis XVI bed. The simple guest room is in a 17th-century Norman manor, the fabric serving as the main decoration and the soft draperies offsetting the austerity of the old tile floor.

The four-poster is the principal decoration in this ► almost bare guest room at Noël Coward's country house. The posts are covered in red velvet, the same fabric that covers the rear panel and serves as a foil for the gay chintz of the tester, the bedspread, and the curtains at the window.

BEDROOMS

▲
To contrast with the busy Chinese wallpaper design in this bedroom, Georges Geffroy chose a large white-lacquered bed, with a headboard covered in old linen velvet and a bedspread of pleated organdy.

◄ The blue and yellow floral print of the English percale curtains and bedstead looks effective against the periwinkle blue walls, while the white, wide-bordered organdy bedspread echoes the white furniture.

Framed by the white-painted wood of a Louis XVI ►
bedstead, the *toile de Jouy* takes on the air of an old engraving. Many elements are combined here to achieve a fin-de-siècle interpretation of Louis XVI: night tables of bronze and glass by Madeleine Castaing, a folding table covered in fringed red velvet by Jacqueline Bruet, a bed by Mercier, and two mahogany tables by Michel Pignères.

In M. Vieljeux's bedroom, the caned bed by Jacob ►
is painted white, and the two wall cabinets are highlighted with white to harmonize with the bed. This use of 18th-century furniture is very well suited to modern living, and the result is a purified version of Louis XVI that makes a perfect background for the picture of a winter landscape.

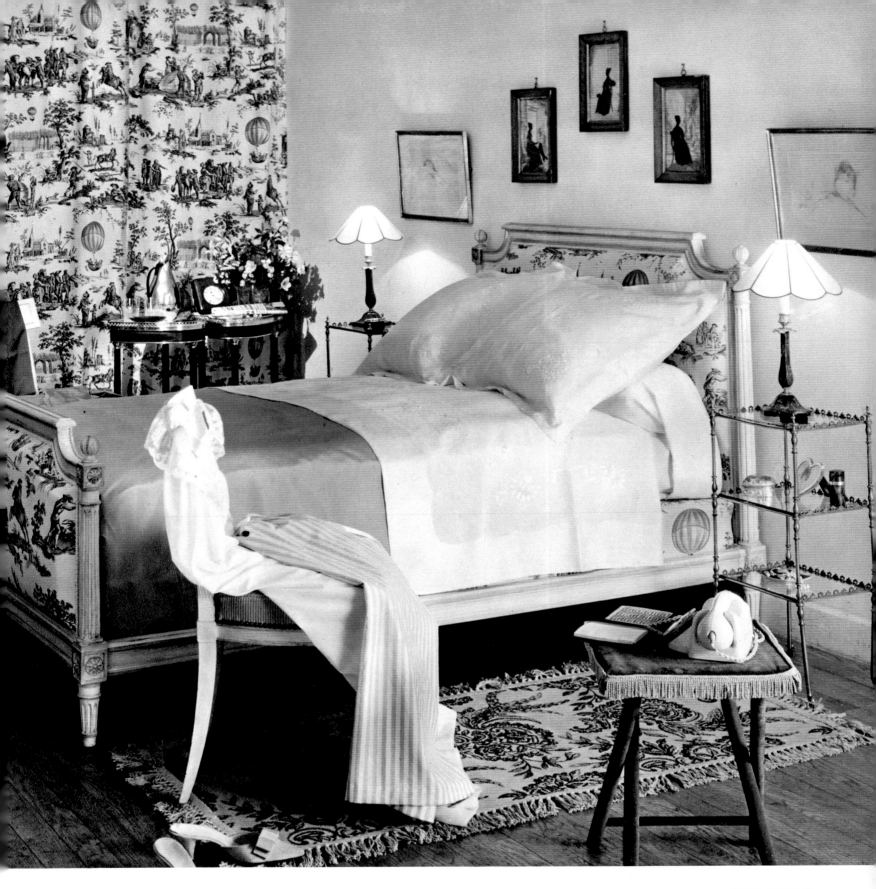

The fashion for white beds

After an eclipse of half a century, white beds are popular again. Their countrified charm has a natural affinity for floral fabrics.

The revival of iron and copper

Their nostalgic appeal carries us back to the days of old-fashioned oil lamps.

◀ The pair of Portuguese beds enlivens the room with its sprightly wrought-iron design. To emphasize the black curlicues, the walls and the alcove were painted a crisp white. The cotton bedspreads are striped in three different shades of blue against a white background and are embroidered with stylized birds and animals. Mme. Etienne decorated this bedroom in M. and Mme. Bleustein-Blanchet's house near Sainte-Maxime.

An Art Nouveau metal bed was ▶ painted black, in the style popular around 1900. The flowing curves of the metal are repeated by the pictures in black and gold frames, hung to form an arch over the headboard. The unconventional color scheme is also of the period. The bed is covered with green English rep, and the pillow and square on the bed were embroidered by the owner in a multicolored flower design on a yellow background, with an appliqué of black lace. The wallpaper has alternating shiny and matte stripes in the same shade of sky blue.

These two guest rooms in the Château de Ferrières were decorated by J. and H. Barroux to evoke memories of the comfortable country guest rooms of two generations ago. The delicate spiral designs of the two romantic copper bedsteads go perfectly with India prints and chintz. ▼

Bedrooms

The everlasting appeal of chintz

In the last ten years, chintz, India prints, and *toile de Jouy* have again demonstrated their appeal both for country rooms and for very feminine rooms.

The linings of old-fashioned ▶ trunks inspired these floral interiors, where bouquets of India prints cover the walls, hang at the windows, and sometimes even cover the ceilings. Here, a blue and white India print is complemented by the blue Greek goatskin rug. In strong contrast are the slipper chair and red-painted floor. The bedspread on the mahogany Louis Philippe sleigh bed is of crisp white cotton.

Flowers abound everywhere in this very feminine bedroom decorated by Dupas. They are on the walls, the ceiling, even on the stool. The floor has soft wall-to-wall carpeting in a solid color, and the bed is covered with a white flounced bedspread.

▼

BEDROOMS

▲
Matching chintz and wallpaper were chosen for this bedroom in a remodeled farmhouse. The rose and gray design appears on the walls, curtains, and bedspread. The white enamel of the 19th-century washstand and the pale gray of the door and the ceiling beams are in harmony with the overall pattern.

◄ In this English interpretation of a romantic bedroom, a Regency tester was given a chintz canopy. Andrée Higgins, the decorator, added a Regency secretary and an overstuffed Victorian slipper chair.

The Second Empire theme is dominant in ▶
this room under the eaves. Mme. Dewavrin painted the walls white and covered the chaise longue and the overstuffed chair with the same rose print used for the curtains. The result suggests a setting for a scene from *Little Women*.

Extra-large beds

They come in many styles, and arranging them attractively in a room requires ingenuity. Big beds are not new, but their use in decoration today is not limited to traditional rooms.

The baroque character of this bedroom, decorated by Philippe Tallien, is due to the magnificent 18th-century Brazilian bed and the shell-back chairs that might almost have been designed by Piranesi. A Provençal throw — white like the walls — serves as a bedspread.

▼

A braid trim can give a smart and dressy look to an oversize bed. The palm-leaf design was the idea of decorator Fred de Cabrol, who also chose the beige wall-to-wall carpeting and solid green curtains, which contribute to the masculine look of the room.

The striking blue and green color scheme is emphasized by the white ▶ wall in this modern bedroom decorated by Dominique Mailliard. Traditional touches are the two 17th-century still lifes that hang on the green silk wall, and the chest of drawers. In sharp contrast are the blue paisley pattern bedspread and the checkered cushion.

The Italian "matrimonio" is used by decorator Pierre Barbe in a simply furnished room. Two Portuguese double beds, placed in an alcove, are joined by a single dyed throw bedspread. The carpeting, slipper chair, walls, and bedspread are all blue to match the colors of the Spanish painting.

▼

BEDROOMS

BEDROOMS

Two beds face each other from opposite ends of a converted attic. The space under the eaves has been utilized for storage cabinets. These are painted white to match the ceiling. Color is provided by the periwinkle blue and white Sicilian carpet and the blue cotton bedspreads with appliquéd bands of white braid which emphasize the straight lines of the bed. At night, a portière of the same blue and white chintz as the curtains can be used to divide the room in two.

◄ By placing two beds head to foot at opposite corners of the room, decorator Roger Lapidouse enables one person to stay awake reading without disturbing the other. The idea is unconventional, but so are the other elements in the room: the wide-striped fabric with turquoise and rose ribbons and flowers, the round table covered with a turquoise felt skirt, and the antique Louis-Philippe side chair.

Beds in pairs

The orthodox arrangement of a pair of beds requires a spacious room, and any other placement requires considerable imagination.

These twin beds are placed side by side in a traditional 18th-century ▶ alcove, originally planned for a single bed. Mme. Étienne, who decorated this bedroom for M. and Mme. Bleustein-Blanchet, chose a palette of light colors: white for the woodwork on the beds, gray and white panelling, and gray curtains with flowered borders. The only strong note is provided by the claret-colored carpeting.

A variation on a country theme: twin beds covered with the same fabric as the curtains. The idea is carried further than usual by covering the box springs with the fabric, too.

The beds in this panelled room were covered with beige cotton to harmonize with the brown woodwork. Wool carpeting in a faded rose color picks up the color of the old brick in the fireplace. The result is saved from being austere by the warm tone of the panelling.
▼

◄ Large areas of color arranged like an abstract painting are the principal decoration in Jacques Damase's study-bedroom. The colors are crisp but not cold. The pale ocher walls dominate over the gray wall-to-wall carpeting, and the whole room is lightened by the white cotton satin curtains and crocheted bedspread. The built-in shelves hold a modern mixture of objects, including old treasures such as the Greco-Roman head a long with new ones. These are almost the only ornaments in a spare but striking décor.

▲ Everyday furnishings, with no brass hardware on the wall cabinets and unpatterned fabrics, were used by decorator Georges Geffroy in this study-bedroom designed for the Vicomte de Bonchamps. The walls are covered with suede-colored canvas. The carpeting is gray, and the curtains are heavy white cotton. The overstuffed sofa is upholstered in chocolate-colored leather, which gives it a sturdy Victorian quality. The fruitwood bureau, too, has a simple vigor, even though it is antique Louis XVI.

Painted walls, solid-color carpeting, and a few handsome ornaments lead to an uncluttered style that is suitably masculine.

BEDROOMS

Study-bedroom for a man 147

For a man:
bedroom-living room

This room is not as austere as a study or as elaborate as a formal living room. The simple furniture and the prints grouped on the walls make a cozy corner for entertaining.

◄ A daybed is the one indispensable piece of furniture in a bedroom-living room. A good choice is a Louis XVI reproduction because it does not look like a real bed. On the advice of decorator Gérard Mille, Raymond Alexandre added some Louis XVI armchairs upholstered in leather and hung his favorite pictures over the bed.

To help bring a long room into better proportion, the Marquis ► de la Bégassière chose a white and charcoal gray *toile de Jouy* for both the walls and the curtains. Here, wall closets eliminate the need for large pieces of furniture. The owner is a hunting and shooting enthusiast, and to decorate the room he has used trophies, guns, hunting knives, and horns. Bright splashes of color are provided by the bed and the armchairs, which are covered in yellow velvet.

BEDROOMS

Leather has a masculine look

Decorator Georges Geffroy created this room for Georges Litman. The use of leather, exotic woods, and solid-color fabrics is very much in fashion.

BEDROOMS

▲
◄ Even the long, full curtains do not detract from the masculine appearance of this room. They are in the same putty-beige fabric that covers the walls. The taffeta undercurtains are ruby red and match the embossed velvet used on the Louis XVI armchairs. Under the windows, the low wainscoting is converted into adjustable louvers that hide the radiators. A "Baigneuse" by Othon Friesz proves that paintings are perfectly appropriate in a functional room. The design of this bed was inspired by an antique example. Despite the tufted upholstery of the Second Empire, the brown leather covering gives it a particularly sturdy appearance. A cushion covered in beige faille, embroidered in ruby red, adds a colorful touch.

The room is free of ornaments. Instead, a decorative effect is ▶ created by the interplay of varied textures and large areas of contrasting colors. The smooth leather on the bed has no embellishment, not even brass studding; the mahogany door with its massive surround and the mahogany frames on the glass closet doors have only the minimum of hardware. The handsome bookcase with panels of beautifully grained mahogany has the same simplicity.

Rooms for children

Floral motifs and strong patterns are a good choice for the young. Sturdy furniture is practical, and built-in cupboards provide uncluttered space.

◀ Seven-year-olds like to have their beds sheltered in a niche. Here the effect has been created by a tester bed hung with white tambour lace. The ceiling of the canopy, the cushion, and the bolster were covered with a cretonne of blue flowers against a bright red background. This was also used for the curtains and the small armchair.

In the same suite of children's rooms, a door to ▶ the room belonging to a three-year-old boy was replaced by a latticework gate. The same lattice was painted on the walls in trompe l'œil, with an imaginary plant growing behind it to complete the illusion. The flowered portières make a charming frame for the doorway, where the two steps are carpeted to soften a fall.

The pleated skirt on this bed hides a trundle bed. The same pattern of blue and green medallions on a white background is used for the wallpaper and the cretonne upholstery. The only piece of furniture used by decorator Serge Royaux was a camphorwood chest that is sturdy, yet has the charm of a provincial Directoire design.

▼

BEDROOMS

◀ A young girl's bedroom is made to look like a living room, and she uses it to entertain her friends. The beribboned wallpaper and the curtain and upholstery fabrics make such a lively decorating scheme that no pictures were needed for the walls.

Popular once again

These rooms echo the character of Louis XVI settings and those of the early 1920s. They need fine furniture, a calculated symmetry, and a lack of clutter.

DINING ROOMS

This house was built in 1925 and decorated at that ▶ time by Jacques Ruhlmann. Serge Royaux left the architecture as it was but has given touches of new life to the décor. There was no need to alter the black, gray, and white marble floor or the brightly lacquered doors by Duna, or the furniture of Macassar ebony and finely grained Amboina wood designed by Ruhlmann. Royaux merely added to the existing grandeur by using white curtains and wall covering of mustard colored raw silk edged with a black fringe.

◀ A Louis XVI style, stripped down to the point of abstraction, was the theme chosen by decorator Emilio Terry for the dining room at the Ermitage de Valbonne in Provence. But the floor gives the room a sumptuous look: rounds of green Alpine marble and squares of red marble from Verona are framed by bands of blue-gray and squares of black Belgian slate. This neo-Palladian arrangement dictated the placement of the small tables.

The return of French styles

After World War II, English dining rooms became the fashion in France. Now French styles of the 18th and 19th centuries are popular again, but subtly changed for modern tastes.

▲

The most important feature in this re-created 18th-century room is the **Louis XVI** panelling, which was painted in a light tone to contrast with the warm wood of the parquet floor. Several tones of terra cotta were used, and the pilasters were marbleized. Decorator **Victor Grandpierre** placed the table and chairs in the exact center of the room, in the traditional manner, and used bronze sconces from the Château de Saint-Cloud to complete the handsome effect.

◄ Mural wallpapers gave **Empire** and **Restoration** dining rooms a delightful air of fantasy without breaking the traditions of earlier styles. But with such a lively background, the rest of the room had to be kept simple. Here, decorator **Fred de Cabrol** has struck an imperial note with gondola chairs and Empire sideboards. The **Dresden** flowers on the chandelier and the floral motifs on the borders of the curtains and in the carpet give the whole room a country air.

A floral wallpaper makes an excellent background for ▶ a mixture of furniture styles. Here the dining table, caned chairs, and the sideboards are all **Louis XVI**. But the **Dumas** wallpaper in white, blue, and cerise has a baroque feeling that is further emphasized by the 19th-century rug of blue ferns bordered in black. A set of white **Sèvres** hounds and wild boars makes a handsome centerpiece.

DINING ROOMS

The freshness of cool colors

In recent years cool colors have grown increasingly popular, especially in dining rooms, where their freshness provides a delightful background at mealtime.

▲
Marbleized walls in white and gray-green, consoles with real Burgundy marble tops, and squares of red and white marble on the floor create a decorative scheme that has the dignity of the 18th-century tradition. Against this austere background each ornament and every detail seem to stand out. The decoration is by Victor Grandpierre for Princess Joseph de Broglie.

In the home of the Marquis and Marquise de la Bégassière, sky-blue ▶ leather was chosen for the upholstery of the fourteen Jean-Baptiste Sée chairs. These were originally ordered from Sée for the National Assembly of 1791. Aside from the mahogany furniture, the gold vermeil and sconces, and the gray marble floor and panelling, blue is the only color used in the room.

Variations on Louis XV

The popularity of the Louis XV style has never diminished. Whether rustic or gilded, it is always effective in dining rooms.

DINING ROOMS

▲
Seven Louis XV Aubusson panels, based on Dumont cartoons taken from Boucher sketches, are the dominant element in M. and Mme. Jacques Abreu's dining room. The walls are covered with gold damask which heightens the blue and strawberry colors of the tapestries. The high-backed Régence chairs are covered with French blue velvet, tufted, and studded with brass nails, and, with the English mahogany table, they add notes of strong, solid color.

◀ **This dining room shows that today liberties are taken even when decorating in the most formal manner. The antique Louis XIV panelling is said to have come from the Hôtel de Gramont, the bust of Mme. de Pompadour by Lemoine decorates a period mantelpiece, the chairs are fine examples of Louis XV, and the mahogany table is Louis Philippe. In a similar manner, the *passementerie* on the valances is of the period, but the solid-color carpet is modern.**

When combined with Louis XVI, Louis XV loses its ▶ baroque heritage, and this is apparent in the room here, for which decorator Georges Geffroy took the theater at Versailles as his theme. The walls are all trompe l'œil: the moldings, the marble, and even the bas-relief panels are in the style of Gabriel. The two sideboards are Louis XVI—handsome pieces in black lacquer and gilt bronze by Weisweiler. The dining table is also Louis XVI, because this was the period in which France adopted once and for all the English concept of the dining room. Again, blue is used—for the chairs and the curtains and in the Agra rug.

New interpretations of the 18th century

Against a plain background, a few fine pieces of Louis XV or Louis XVI furniture can recall the style without re-creating a true period room.

◀ Modern ideas have been incorporated into this interpretation of an 18th-century dining room created by Mrs. Burrall Hoffman. The rose-colored fabric on the wall is in typical Louis XV color, but no designer of that period would have made a horizontal panel of it and then underlined it with a low white dado. The Régence chairs covered with pastel green and gold fabric surround a copy of a fine and delicate Louis XVI table.

◀ Warm colors can be used successfully in a formal room. At the Château Lintôt-les-Bois, Serge Royaux used tobacco-colored fabric for the walls and curtains, and he put a moss-green carpet on the floor. Against this background we see a mixture of simple 18th-century pieces: English chairs, a Louis XVI sideboard, and a table in the style of the Consulate.

The decor of this dining room is of the 1880s, but ▶ J. and H. Barroux have given it an air of fres ness that is in direct contrast to the fussiness of the period. The cane-back chairs with carved legs, the molding on the panelling, and the sideboard in the Henri II style are all typical of the era, but the usual heavy curtains have been replaced by a chintz.

The Duchesse d'Harcourt's dining room under ▶ the eaves has a bare but attractive simplicity. The walls are painted, and the tile floor is like many found in old Paris town houses. There is no elaboration; even the fine Louis XV chairs are covered in a solid-color velvet. There is no marquetry in the room, and the only veneers are on the table and the Louis XVI mahogany sideboards. Instead of an Oriental carpet, the rug chosen is plain, except for a simple Greek key border.

DINING ROOMS

Three romantic rooms

Ideas for those who dislike solemn dining rooms.

Eclectic romanticism. Only an incurable romant with a taste for the unusual could put rustic, rush-seated, Provençal chairs in the dining room of a huge old manor house, a series of vases of flowers on the pull-out shelves of a bookcase instead of piling up books and papers, and Max Ernst's "Portuguese Nun" on the wall of such an antique setting.

◀ Period romanticism. The general theme of the 19th century was sufficiently established in this dining room to allow for the introduction of a fine Charles X rug and antique Napoleon III chairs. The dining table by Jansen was inspired by the period. Princess Caetani chose it because it went well with the chairs and was also eminently practical. Its black synthetic surface is proof against almost all accidents, and the extra leaves stretch it out to a length of over six feet.

Atmospheric romanticism. This stems from the light- ▶ ing and from the combination of different materials. The dining room was created by the American sculptor Herbert Haseltine for his Paris house. In the evening a romantic aura invades this lovely room, where everything is 18th century. The panelling is Louis XV, as are the caned armchairs, and the French 18th-century glass chandelier, the Louis XV sconces, and the candelabra shed a soft candlelight over the muted colors—lilac and very pale green—of the panelling, and on the terra-cotta of the antique tiles. The mahogany surface of the Louis XVI table and the old rose silk of the Austrian shades glow softly.

DINING ROOMS

DINING ROOMS

◄ The dining room in the Château d'Acqueville (owned by M. and Mme. C. de Lassuchette) is in the style of an old farm. The cherrywood table and the rush-seated Directoire chairs are uncompromisingly rustic, as are the red tile floor and the waxed oak timbers. Only the niches that hold pottery betray the sophistication of the city-dweller.

In the cellar of the Château ▶ d'Épone, the half-rustic dining room with its 12th-century vaulting is a reflection of past centuries: the Middle Ages evoked by the rooster, once a church weathervane, the age of Louis XIII when the present château was built, and the period when part of the château was a Masonic temple, visited by Benjamin Franklin. The decoration has been reduced to a minimum, but each piece adds to the effect: the farmhouse table and benches, the iron pot, the bottle rack that could be taken as Pop Art, and the reflected light.

In a country house decorated by Jean Dive, the tradition of a farmhouse dining room has been faithfully adhered to. The long table and oak chairs belong to no particular period but have an ageless rustic solidity. The chairs are covered in bright blue velvet, the walls are beige cotton, and the antique red tiles on the floor provide the major color accent in the room.

▼

Rustic simplicity

Country dining rooms can be placed anywhere, even in the cellar, but the important thing is not the finish of the walls but the right choice of materials together with simple, rustic furniture.

KITCHENS

The functional kitchen

A kitchen that is solely for cooking can be made to look less clinical by the choice of interesting materials for the walls and floors.

A fabric in a mosaic pattern designed by Paule Marrot was chosen by Jean Royère to cover the walls of this kitchen. Designed ten years ago, the fabric foreshadows Op Art, and here it has been laminated to make it practical for kitchen use. The same material was used in its plain, unlaminated form as hangings at the windows and doors. The "Dalami" tiles on the floor are in a solid color which avoids the conflict that a checkerboard pattern would create with the hexagonal design on the walls.

◄ Here, terra-cotta tiles are used on the walls as well as on the floor. Their dull surface and subtle coloring have a special appeal for those who like old-fashioned kitchens, but they also go very well with the modern stainless steel counter-top and hood. The varnished pine cabinets look handsome, and they are practical, too, with the minimum of ornamentation. The built-in television is evidence that it is possible to relax in the kitchen — and this keeps the cook happy.

Small, glazed, oblong tiles create a pattern ► over the long work counter in this modern kitchen. Tiles are practical as well as attractive, for they cut down the glare that would come from a white wall. Combined with the cabinets of varnished oak, they contribute to the countrified air, while the panelled cabinet doors add an antique look. The white "Polyrey" on the counters goes well with the wood and the dark green walls. The ceramic tile floor is a muted gray.

Areas for cooking and eating

The most successful kitchen — dining rooms have a sophisticated simplicity, and they never betray how much they owe to modern appliances.

THE KITCHEN

The authentic look of this kitchen remodeled by Max ▶
Brusset in the Château d'Épone demonstrates a major
trend in today's decoration. The old is carefully preserved and the modern is cleverly disguised. The old
beams were retained, and the cabinets were decorated
with painted wooden panels that date from the end of the
16th century. No plastic is used: the counter-top and
splashboard are tile, and so is the floor. The walls are
whitewashed, in the traditional way, and brick shelves
are used for ornamentation.

◀ The old-fashioned look in Frederick Stagg's kitchen
betrays the hand of a master chef. He has created his
decorating scheme around the tools of the trade—both
antique and modern—that he has accumulated throughout the years. Over the fireplace are shelves to hold
cookbooks, and below these hangs a collection of copper
utensils that gleam in front of the old polychrome tiles.
Oriental rugs and Louis XVI chairs and table make it clear
that this room was planned just as much for eating as
it was for cooking.

The rustic look of this kitchen designed by Comera ▶
stems from peasant traditions, despite the fact that
some of the materials and equipment show a highly
sophisticated taste. The cabinets are teak. The cooking
top is set in an olive-green laminated counter-top. Above
this is a hood with an exhaust fan — not the usual hood
blackened by time, but a shiny, stainless steel one. The
area that would be the fireplace in a real farmhouse
kitchen is covered with small glazed ceramic tiles. The
woodbox has been converted into a bin for storing wine.
The hearth holds a built-in Scholtès oven, and above
it is a barbecue. There is every modern convenience,
in fact, yet the country look remains.

In the farmhouse idiom

As equipment gets more and more modern, the appearance of kitchens becomes more antique. To day the idea is to recapture the feeling of an old farm.

The country theme inspires dining kitchens of seductive charm. Pierre Barbe has painted the walls and cabinets of his own kitchen to simulate knotty pine and put terracotta tiles on the floor. The oven, which recalls the old country kitchen stoves, is faced with geometric brown and white tiles. Above the oven door, controls for the three top burners are mounted on a brass pipe in the old-fashioned manner. At the left, above the drawer for warming plates, a rotisserie with an electric spit is set over a wood fire, revealing how traditional equipment is modernized yet keeps its antique appearance. The Louis XIII table and chairs testify that style counts as much as function.

A more rugged look suited the kitchen of the hunting lodge ▶ that Pierre Barbe designed at Ypres (see pages 82-83). The concept is that of a very old farmhouse; the equipment comes from contemporary manufacturers. At right, the oven (which is above a warming oven that has humidity controls to make it easy to keep meals hot) is set into a jog in the wall such as one often finds in country houses. To the left, a Giraudon rotisserie (with a motor in the storage cupboard to its right) has a truly traditional look. The furniture is both simple and rustic : a modern serving and work table designed by Pierre Barbe, an old farmhouse dining table and chairs that are sturdy copies of old ones.

THE KITCHEN

Two rooms that are not quite separate

These kitchens are a compromise between the separate kitchen for cooking and the kitchen used for eating.

▲
The cabinet-divider that does not reach all the way up to the ceiling can still conceal the major working areas of the kitchen from the area reserved for eating. It also adds useful wall space to the kitchen without sacrificing the feeling of spaciousness or continuity of the white-washed walls. In her farmhouse (see pages 238-241), Mme. Van Leyden has also added a bar counter with fixed stools where quick snacks can be served.

◄ Hanging cabinets can also serve as a partition. Here they are suspended over a pass-through counter on two prefabricated beams. Space was limited in this Saint-Cloud apartment, so the pass-through does double duty as a dining table. Its top is laminated plastic, under which there are small drawers and pigeonholes for extra storage. The result is a complete kitchen-dining area neatly fitted into a small space.

▲
A partial storage wall can be used to interrupt the monotony of a long, narrow room. And it has the practical advantage of providing storage space right at the point of use. In this kitchen, designed by Alfred Bernard, the unit, distributed by Universal-Mesure, has a serving counter on the kitchen side and several cabinets with grained plastic doors on the dining side. Sliding glass panels can be pushed back to make a pass-through at mealtime. The flooring of ceramic tile gives a sense of unity to the two areas.

A free-standing counter is sufficient to separate a small ▶ kitchen from the dining area. This is especially true if the counter is designed with the same care as real furniture. This one by Ecolux has beautifully grained teak doors and a marble top. The large armoire in the background, which helps to hide the kitchen, contains a broom closet on the kitchen side, a clothes closet on the corridor side, and a refrigerator on the third side.

◄ This counter of warm, waxed brick almost has the effect of joining the kitchen and dining area instead of dividing them. In a country kitchen designed by Serge Royaux, the work area is really in an alcove at one end of the room. The white walls of the dining area set off the colors, but the two areas are joined by the green and white wallpaper on the ceiling and the black and white floor tiles.

A storage counter provides a larger work area than most tables, and it is certainly much sturdier. It also saves space, as utensils can be housed in it when not in use. In Mme. Bouchayer's country house (see pages 60-63), Serge Royaux shows how a storage counter can look decorative. It is covered with unglazed stoneware tiles and the sides are sheathed with the same white panelling used on the walls.

Rooms that are hardly separate

Work counters create a separation that is more visual than real.

BATHROOMS

The look of the boudoir

Lined like a 19th-century chest, sparkling with mirrors, today's bathrooms no longer resemble sterile laboratories.

A blue floral pattern fabric ▶ covers the walls of this bathroom under the eaves, making it seem like the extension of a bedroom. The fixtures are also blue, which makes a glamorous change from the customary white. The shirred skirts on the dressing table and stool and the vase of flowers emphasize the feeling of a Second Empire boudoir.

◀ **Blue Portuguese tiles** cover the walls, floor, and ceiling of this bathroom by **Georges Geffroy**. The only thing that separates the bathroom and the adjoining dressing room is the bathtub in the alcove. The living-room look is derived from the wall of **Louis XV** closets, with shirred taffeta behind the glass doors. These were inspired by the décor in Mme. du Barry's private apartments at Versailles. The **Louis XV** armchair and the **Louis XVI** side chair emphasize the style.

For small bathrooms the ▶ country look is ideal. Here it is achieved by using a red tile floor and checked fabric. Panes of glass cover the fabric where necessary.

The combination of fabric and wood looks well in bathrooms, as elsewhere. But it is wise to shield the fabric with glass next to the bathtub and to enamel the wood to protect it from moisture. Standing in front of the rose and gray Directoire fabric is a charming 19th-century bathtub decorated by a silken cord and tassels looped through eyes. Wall-to-wall nylon carpeting covers the tile floor, enhancing the boudoir feeling.

◀ A mixture of many different elements helps to create the living-room look. Alain Demachy has followed this concept as far as it can go in this bathroom created for the Comtesse de Brantes. The walls are covered with real chintz and topped by a real cornice of a kind not usual in bathrooms. The washbasin fitted into a cabinet with moldings makes one think of Louis XVI furniture. The dressing table covered in Swiss muslin (protected, of course, by a sheet of glass) is lit by Louis XV lamps, and the chair is Louis XVI. Even marquetry makes its appearance in the form of a small Louis XV bookcase, the final touch in the metamorphosis of an erstwhile utilitarian room.

THE BATH - SITTING ROOM ▲

Function seems to have been spirited away. Wallpapered like the walls and the ceiling, the tub in this bathroom decorated by Mme Livingstone looks like some sort of banquette. The other fixtures have disappeared from this little room. The skirted dressing table, the Second Empire mirror with its gilt gesso frame reveal the urge to banish at all cost anything that recalls the bathroom. A small mahogany Louis-Philippe bureau, of which one gets barely a glimpse, and family portraits testify that this is a private retreat as much as a functional bathroom.

One can go further : furnished and decorated with prints, the bathroom can be a private retreat.

Plastic-treated fabrics

The selection now available offers every kind of style, such as a tent in the Charles X manner and a rotunda inspired by the 18th century.

▲
It takes considerable skill to use a single motif successfully, but decorator **Pierre Delbée** of the firm of Jensen has shown how it can be done in his own bathroom. The same fabric is used throughout — a blue and white "Taco" percale decorated with stripes of stylized foliage that was inspired by Empire and Restoration borders. The ceiling is covered so that it looks like the roof of a tent, and the cornice is simply a trompe l'œil effect created with a strip of the fabric placed horizontally at the top of the wall. Even the sides of the bathtub are sheathed in this treated fabric. A white opaline chandelier gives the final touch to this **Charles X** fantasy.

◄ The graceful folds of full-length curtains and wall-to-wall carpeting are possible, thanks to the special treatment of fabrics with splash-resistant plastic. When there is enough space, the placement of the bathtub under the window is an attractive idea, as displayed by decorator **Georges Ottin** in this circular bathroom.

Pink was chosen as the basic color for this bathroom created by ▶ **Pierre Delbée.** The pink of the fixtures is matched by the pink in the treated wall fabric and in the towels. In addition, pink molding surrounds the medicine cabinet, the niche with glass shelves, and the tub alcove. Occasional stripes of pink were incorporated into the floor.

BATHROOMS

    Unusual effects with wood and slate

▲
A bathroom featuring wood and fabric can have a romantic intimacy that is particularly well suited to a chalet or cabin. Here the bathtub is fitted in tight against the log wall, with its outside sheathed in matching wood. No ornament—nothing superfluous—competes with the wood walls in this décor by **Jacques Luzeau.**

François Crahay made no attempt to hide the fact that this ▶ is an attic, and he turned it into a bathroom of great character. Not only did he leave the original timbers alone, but he added matching wooden boards on the walls, from the wainscoting right up to the ceiling. The wainscoting is actually a continuation of the ceramic tile floor. A Second Empire stool and a neo Louis XVI mirror of the same period are in the same witty vein as the printed parody of a leopard-skin rug that decorates the center of the floor.

Wood and slate are the basic materials for nonconformist bathrooms in the country and in town, whether they resemble an attic or a sparkling jewel box.

◄ **Polished wood planks cover the walls of this small, compact bathroom. Any feeling of monotony is overcome by the burnished brass sconces, the mirror frame, and the prints hung on the wall. A cabinet under the washbasin ingeniously hides a towel rack as well as a bidet that is attached to the plumbing by a flexible pipe.**

▲

Slate and brass create the unusual blend of color and texture in this bathroom. Strips of yellow brass accentuate the matte surface of the slate that was used for the floor, the walls, and even the invisible cabinet doors. The gray-blue of the fixtures brings out the brilliance of the gilt-bronze faucets, sconces, and glass-holders, all of which have a turtle design.

A handsome small bathroom worked out entirely in gray ► and white. It has slate flooring, slate walls for two-thirds of their height, and slate outside the tub. The upper part of the walls and the ceiling are white.

They have the universality of established values. The irregular hues of these large terra-cotta tiles would not be out of place in the days of Louis XIV. But they are also unsophisticated enough to go well with a simple fabric. Serge Royaux drew the double conclusion: in this authentic Louis XIV chateau he would hang curtains to give privacy to the bathtub and he would choose a coarse fabric suite to the purpose and then drape it in the most classic manner, repeating the happy choice of this same material at the window.

They have the grandeur of a noble material. Fred de Cabrol used them as wainscoting in a house designed by René Part, in which the age of Louis XIII gave the inspiration. As a background for the blue fixtures, the dull tones of the clay glaze resemble the patina of centuries. A point to remember : the soft glow of terra cotta suits bathrooms of vast proportions in which modern ceramic tiles would be too glossy and bright.

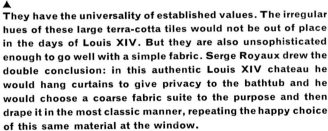 They are of ancient lineage. These Provençal tiles are direct descendents of medieval designs. Their antique appearance goes extremely well with the usually irregular proportions of old rooms that one wants to remodel into bathrooms. Here the hues which go from ocher to green and from green to yellow, shrewdly mixed by decorator Androuchka, give a warm patina with the glamour of ancient manors in the bathroom.

Variations in terra cotta

For those who like patina, subtle shadings and a whiff of the antique, terra-cotta tiles have the virtue of tradition and the good qualities of an eternally modern material.

Marble
real and synthetic

Victor Grandpierre shows how marble can be used today to create bathrooms in the grand manner.

▲
Panelling framed by mahogany molding gives solemn splendor to Yves Lanvin's bathroom, which was designed by Victor Grandpierre. A royal red marble surrounds both the washbasin and the bathtub and appears again in squares in the floor. The adjoining dressing room has the same panelling on the walls, but the floor has wall-to-wall carpeting.

◄ **The imperial tradition inspired Victor Grandpierre's decoration for ▶ Mme. Yves Lanvin's bathroom. The floor is tiled with squares of white Carrara marble alternating with rose-colored Bavarian marble. The Bavarian marble is also used around the bathtub and washbasin. On the walls, the panelling is outlined with rose-colored marbleized strips, which become lighter in shade toward the ceiling. The dolphin faucets and the gilt-bronze sconces are faithful to the Empire period. The Empire armchair and stools make the room seem like a boudoir, and to further this illusion, the washbasin has a silk skirt, and the dressing table across the room is covered with embroidered batiste. This is protected by a glass tabletop. The curtains at the bathtub alcove are silk, lined on the inside with rose-colored plastic. A toilet set in blond tortoise shell and bottles in crystal and silver seem like fine bibelots, and on the wall, marble and plaster medallions suit the formal decoration perfectly.**

BATHROOMS

The gamut of ceramic tile

Tile is one of the oldest materials invented by man, and its delightful qualities are as popular as ever. Here it is used successfully with trompe l'œil effects and skillful lighting,

▲
Tiles set into solid-color plaster panels are scattered over the walls of this bathroom in a way that derives from both trompe l'œil and "pop art." More tiles are nailed to the cabinet which holds a water heater.

▲
On the floor of this spacious bathroom glazed "Clausonnes" tiles outlined with white make a sinuous pattern that is in direct contrast with the rectilinear pattern on the walls. There is an even greater contrast between the intense ultramarine that architect André Svetchine chose for the floor and the light yellow "Apt" wall tiles.

Romanticism in the modern idiom is based here on trompe-l'œil and the evocative power of color. Two shades of pink were chosen for the wall tiles, which create the illusion of a striped fabric. The fixtures in a darker shade of pink blend smoothly into the color scheme. Both the tiles and fixtures are by Selles.

A flight of seagulls against a background of different ▶ shades of blue seems to add height and an airy lightness to the walls of this bathroom decorated by Mme. Petis-Dugrenot. She followed this same theme (a recommendation of Nils Olgersson) with the ceiling lights, which suggest gaps of sunlight in a cloudy ocean sky. For the bathtub and the floor, small, square, glazed tiles in a deep marine blue were used.

BATHROOMS

A mosaic of small, glazed, blue and white tiles runs in ▶ stripes across the floor, up the side of the bathtub, and then right up to the window in Jean Royère's bathroom at Marly-le-Roi. On the walls, a yellow and white plastic-treated fabric offers a contrast of narrower, paler stripes.

Terra-cotta and glazed tiles create a pink and blue chessboard where the matte texture of one is enhanced by the glossy brilliance of the other. For the shower walls and floor, Philippe Tallien chose monochrome tiles in a bright Mediterranean blue.

An entire wall of "Cerabati" tiles suggests an old-fashioned wallpaper, but it is richer and more practical. This remodeled bathroom is built under the eaves of Sacha Distel's chalet. A wall lamp covered with an opaline shade is a romantic touch.
▼

BATHROOMS

▲
The dividing line between the bathroom and the garden is almost invisible in this house decorated by Pierre Barbe. The tub of travertine rises from the floor and appears to be simply a stepping-stone to the landscape. There is nothing to clutter up a view which has as its principal ornament the treetops that appear at the edge of the terrace. The horsehead spout overlooks the tub to give a surrealist accent and the birdbath outside further mixes make-believe and real.

◄ The garden invades the bathroom, held in check only by sliding panes of glass between the window and the tub. A chessboard of tiles in two shades of yellow serves as flooring, covers the sides and edges of the tub and spreads out on the walls behind the green plants to emphasize a spatial continuity. In the rest of the bathroom, a flowered decorating scheme stops sharply at the shower curtains, as though the latter were the division between a boudoir and a garden. For the washbasins, Jacques Luzeau chose a style inspired by the 19th century to enclose them in a cabinet made of marble.

Bathrooms with gardens

Even for this most private of rooms, the dividing line between indoors and outdoors can be breached. Either the garden comes indoors, or the house opens to the outdoors—with a few precautions.

▲

In a small space, decorator Jacques Luzeau has created an imaginary vista. Between the bathtub and the wall and behind curtains parted by tiebacks, he built a planter in which two fig trees and a fern are placed. This small, four-foot box of plants suggests a view over a garden. "Herbier" tiles by Capron complete the theme.

The main feature of this marble and glass bathroom is the border of plants at the base of the window-wall and the view of the lawn and trees through the glass wall and ceiling. The result is as handsome as the modern living rooms now being designed by American and Scandinavian architects.

◄ There is an abstract purity about this white and gold bathroom. The sunken bathtub of white ceramic tiles gives an unobstructed view of the sheltered courtyard, landscaped with green plants. The intervening wall is of insulating glass to keep the bathroom warm.

The ancient barn of an 18th century country house has become M. and Mme Pierre Delbée's summer dining room. The decorator has left the uneven patina of the rough-plaster walls alone and covered the old beams with a ceiling of rattan. For greater comfort, the stone bench along the wall was covered with cushions of gray canvas. They are held in place by a rope that passes through brass rings cemented into the wall. The red cushions propped on the 19th century black iron chairs create a unity of color.

Open on three sides, Philippe Tallien's terrace at Saint-Tropez extends out from the house and is sheltered by rattan and climbing plants. The mixed air of country freshness and elegance is due quite simply to the potted plants that edge the terrace and to the blue and white of the tablecloth, the chairs and the plates.

TERRACES

They have a rustic air and protect one against too much sun, all one can ask for in areas where there is no need to fear a sudden torrential downpour.

Rattan for shelter in Provence

TERRACES

Hanging gardens

Every Parisian dreams of a roof-garden.

Since a real lawn would be impratical because of the danger of water, seeping through to the floor below, many city-dwellers substitute plastic lawn-carpets. But the shrubs and flowers in tubs can be real.

The plant beds (above, opposite), built of dressed stone, have added height to provide ample soil for the flowers and the climbing plants that grow up the reed fence. Exotic touches are provided by the curvilinear straw rug, the elaborate basket-work chair, and the brass-topped Moorish table. In the foreground are shish kebabs for a barbecue.

◄ A low border of shrubbery is just high enough to give privacy, yet allows the fine panoramic view of Paris to be seen from the terrace. A garden path runs around this room at the top of the house, with the stone flagging underfoot. The shrubs grow in concrete planters of different heights so as to avoid any feeling of uniformity and to simulate natural growth. As an extra precaution the planters are held firmly in place with iron bars.

Trellises with climbing shrubs give the impression of an old- ► fashioned walled garden. The shrubs grow in concrete plant-ers, which are also placed along the railing, to hold low shrubs and flowers. The design was worked out by Mme. Lefebvre-Vilardebo.

TERRACES

Three ways to plan a terrace

Part of this terrace in a house on the Côte des Maures is shaded by an awning of white canvas. The linear harmony of the decoration, planned by Mme. Planus, is seen in the geometric pattern of the "Apt" tiles underfoot and the stylized foliage of the white wrought-iron furniture. The same curlicues appear in the wicker chairs in the background.

◀ An extended eave of a country house makes an ideal shelter for this small terrace. The effect here is of an old, overgrown barn. The rough surfaces of the hand-hewn beams were carefully preserved, and a hop plant was allowed to grow right up the wall. Light and simple bamboo furniture was a perfect choice for this cool, rustic setting.

A boathouse on the bank of the Seine was converted into a cottage, and the veranda was transformed into a summer living — dining room. The canvas curtains shelter the veranda from light winds and too much morning sun. ▶

It is important to be in the open air, but also to provide the right kind of shelter for the climate.

A garden-living room

On the roof of a Paris house Victor Grandpierre and the Vicomte de Noailles have created a green folly that reflects the 18th century.

TERRACES

This terrace makes a real living room, for it has the right plan and charming, lightly scaled furniture. Mme. Jean Ralli uses it for parties during the Paris season. The bust of a Roman emperor is the focal point for a décor of antique Directoire chairs made of black wrought iron and wooden slats painted green. The terra-cotta plant tubs that hold small trees also look like collector's items. This is also a real garden, with shrubs planted at the bottom of a trellised niche. Ivy and hop plant, mugho pines, dwarf Japanese cedars, pyracanthas and cotoneasters, topiary boxwood in spheres and cones are combined to make a splendid show. The entire terrace is covered with grass — a plastic lawn that comes in squares. Beyond the trellises is the handsome dome of the Hôtel des Invalides and a superb panorama of the city.

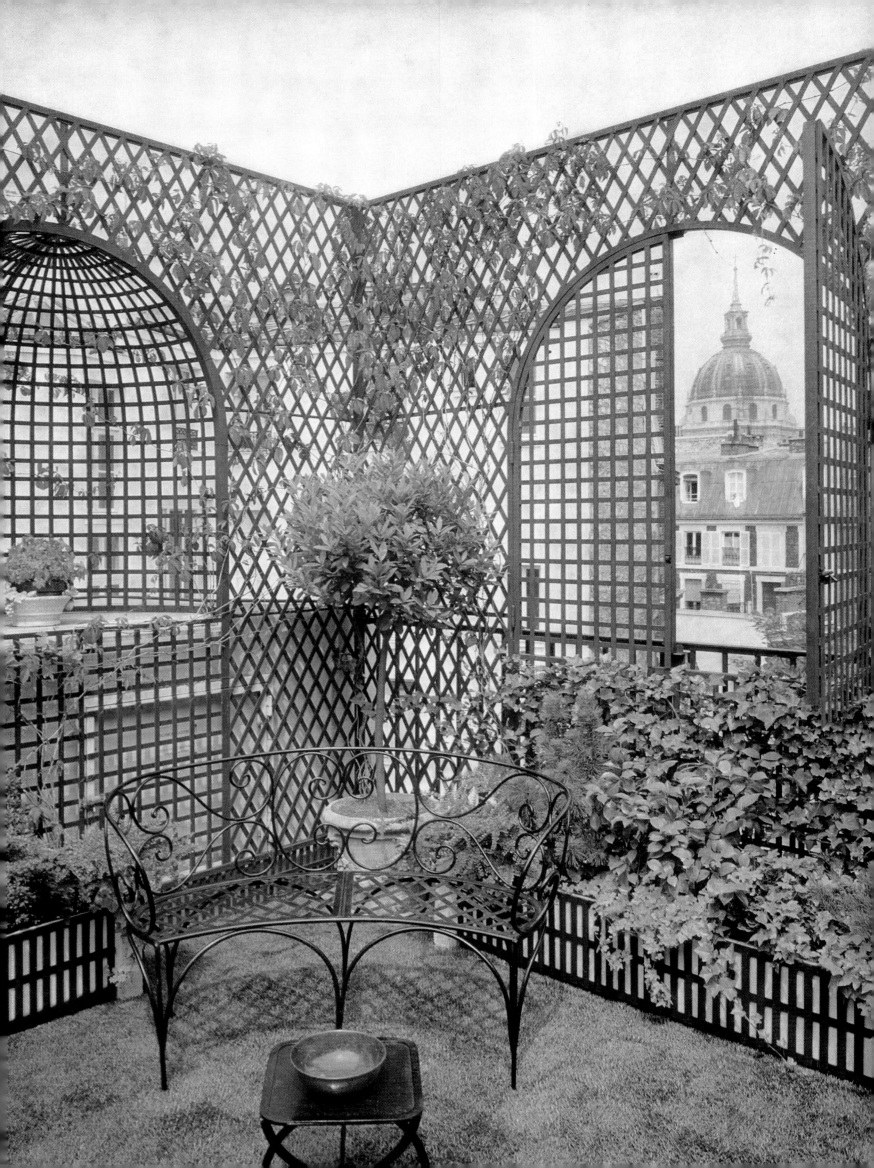

The rather forbidding ashlar walls of this terrace were softened with straw mats, and the result has something of the air of a romantic ruin. The painter Vidal-Quadras emphasizes the idea of ruins with his design for the far end of the terrace.

A windbreak of half-round timbers on the eighth floor ▶ of a house at Porte Saint-Cloud (on the outskirts of Paris) makes this terrace look like a log cabin. The natural form of the coffee table and the basketwork of the chair and the stools have an equally primitive quality. The designers were Hervé Baley and Dominique Zimbacca.

Low undulating walls of dressed stone contribute an air of fantasy to this terrace designed by Gérard Bourdariat in collaboration with the landscape architect, M. Veyret. The zigzag pattern of the crazy paving makes an amusing contrast with the gently curving lines of the plant beds that enclose the terrace on all sides.

▼

TERRACES

Terrace architecture

Today's terraces follow the modern trend for straight forward materials and free-form shapes.

A COUNTRY
BOUQUET

Millhouses and barns in old villages, with their weathered tiles and ancient walls, have a picturesque simplicity. Most of them need to be touched up rather than decorated. With repainted walls and moldings, pretty curtains, country furniture, and a few simple but distinguished objects, the rooms can be livable and charming.

19TH-CENTURY ECHOES

This building, on a narrow lane in the old part of Saint-Tropez, has the same faded pink exterior as the paving stones. The alfresco dining room (page 195) is under the vine-covered trellis.

Philippe Tallien's house at Saint-Tropez

The house seems to emerge from a grove of laurels and yew trees. The interior of the three-story structure is entirely white, accented by floors of terra-cotta tiles and old, checked beams that have darkened with age. The owner-decorator has gone to great lengths to avoid decorating in a set period or manner. Fine furniture is used throughout the house, but by mixing periods Philippe Tallien has avoided the impression of a museum of antiques. The study on the main floor was obviously inspired by the era of Louis Philippe, and the rooms upstairs range from a 17th-century bedroom to an 18th-century living room. As a result, there is a subtle modulation of atmosphere from room to room. Throughout the house there is an air of 19th-century bourgeois prosperity which, when handled with M. Tallien's skill, has a totally unexpected and seductive charm. Part of his skill has been in keeping down the number of ornaments and avoiding an excess of tassels and frills — so that the 19th-century spirit is not overwhelming.

▲

A bust of Caesar stands between two Roman amphorae salvaged from the sea, and the set of marine water colors on the white plaster wall are of the Toulon squadron in 1870.

◀ Several of the works in the study (opposite and right) are by well- ▶ known artists and add a light-hearted quality to the room. One of the thoroughbred portraits is by A. Adams, and the plaster horse's head over the arched doorway is by Carpeaux. The handsome, but never solemn, background consists of white walls, red curtains, a tile floor patterned with small squares, and 19th-century mahogany furniture.

19TH-CENTURY ECHOES *continued*

▲
Beautiful pieces of furniture do not lessen the freshness of this deceptively simple décor. On the floor, tiles from Aix create a terra-cotta covering inspired by the Middle Ages. In front of the 17th-century English desk is a 16th-century Florentine stool made of brass and wrought iron. The 19th-century Canton china lamp and the portrait of the owner painted by the local Saint-Tropez artist Vachon add further to the mixture of styles.

◄ Antique balusters are the principal ornament of this provincial staircase, but on the mahogany Empire table there is a collection of potted plants, and, on the wall, a row of sketches by Beaudinière. These are all elements that could be used successfully to enhance a landing in any country house.

Bright, tropical colors used on furniture of imposing scale and the ▶ glowing colors of the Restoration portrait at one end of the room give unusual vigor to the decoration of the living room. The full, pleated wall hangings of dull red satin run right up to the white ceiling. The black Louis XIV desk and the armchairs covered in green velvet stand out sharply against the blue and beige Isfahan rug. The more muted tones of the wooden chest and the dark ceiling beams keep the play of colors from being overpowering.

Walls of light-colored brick partly covered with stucco, a stone chimney, and old tiles on the roof contribute to the timeless quality of this country dwelling

A REMODELED BARN
For week-ends near Paris

Basically this is a new house, skillfully planned by decorator Jean Dive, but it resembles partly the old barn that it once was and partly the manor house that served as a model for the new design. The result is the kind of architecture that suits both a vacation house and a year-round residence. It is fitted with every modern convenience, and has a swimming pool and pool house. In the vacation mood are the white-painted beams in the living room and the terra-cotta tile floors;

the stuffed deer head recalls a week-end of hunting. In the same vein are the 19th-century prints and the happy combination of 17th-century pieces mixed with provincial furniture of the 19th century. But there are also elements typical of a more formal year-round house, such as the fine details, the embossed velvet upholstery, and the delicate veneered furniture. Thus the house provides the solid comfort sought by most city-dwellers when they go out to the country.

Gothic doors of waxed wood and carved arches, or doors painted white and decorated with iron nailheads, evoke memories of old manor houses. They also blend the real Middle Ages with the romantic 19th-century Gothic revival.

Russell Page designed these lawn gardens on different levels. Between them, low walls lined with flowers act as dividers. The old flagstones on the paths, the design of the pool house, and the pool itself are all so cleverly understated that the luxurious effect is minimized.

◀ **Arches of old beams form a rhythmic pattern in the long bedroom hall.**

▲
Still lifes composed of dried plants fill two niches. On either side of the steps, simple country chairs help to fill the wall space. The view here is toward the living room, which is shown on the next two pages.

▲
Certain characteristics remind us continually of an old building. One such quality is lack of symmetry. Here a single beam near one end of the bedroom has been used to mark off an alcove. There is a shuttered door at one end of it, and a glass-panelled door at the other. On the captain's chest the white china statuette of Dr. Livingstone is mounted as a lamp to symbolize not only the 19th-century but also the English influence, both of which were important in the decoration of the house.

Country decoration in a romantic mood is the theme in this simple bedroom. ▶
The ceiling is divided by a single massive beam. The black walnut chest is Louis Philippe, and the rug, in a Restoration design, makes a cheerful contrast to the terra-cotta tiles.

17th and 19th centuries blend here without clashing, due to the strong background of bottle-green fabric which covers the walls and because no attempt was made to create a period room. Five English prints hang over a Spanish table, Louis XIII chairs stand next to a Gothic Revival door, and there is a convenient folding table next to the sofa.

A REMODELED BARN *continued*

As in a remodeled barn, the basic ornaments of this living room are the exposed beams, roughhewn and wrinkled with age, that have been painted white to lighten them. The walls and the ceiling are covered with green fabric to match the curtains and valances. The 17th century white stone fireplace is raised on a stone base is the focal point of the room around which comfortable sofas are gathered.

IN THE 19TH-CENTURY MANNER
A house with every comfort

This residence was originally a farm. Today, it has been converted into a comfortable house for country week-ends. The long white façade, tile roof, and nearby pond for watering the stock were retained. On the inside, the existing plan was also left alone, except for the tearing down of one wall, which resulted in the creation of a superb long room instead of two smaller rooms. This area serves as living room, front hall, and dining room, the different areas being marked off by the massive cross-beams in the ceiling. To soften the stark white of the ceiling and yet not darken the room too much, the spaces between the beams were painted a pale blue, and from a distance these look like faint shadows. The expanse of the walls was also broken by covering them with a cotton pekin in white and putty-colored stripes. A false rusticity would be out of keeping with the present use of the house. In fact, innumerable details betray the sophistication of the city-dweller, such as the huge Persian rug that adds warmth to the room, the built-in bookshelves on either side of the fireplace, and the fruitwood furniture. But even these elements have been used simply and blend with the contemporary furniture, the lack of ornamentation, and the solid-color fabrics. It has all the comfort that is associated with the word "home," which is what Mme. Luisita Price wanted.

▲
Under the eaves, the beams and ribs of the house stand out dramatically. In the master bedroom, they are seen against a background of pink moire wallpaper. A printed cotton with pink roses and gray foliage was used for the curtains and sleeping alcove, on the Second Empire slipper chair, and for the bedspread on the Napoleon I bed. The chest of drawers is also Napoleon I and holds late-19th-century ornaments that are typical of country houses.

In a romantic alcove, a walnut sleigh bed is tucked in behind the timbers. The contrast between the hand-hewn wood of the timbers and the polished wood of the furniture is particularly striking against the lively wallpaper. ▶

◀ Muted fabrics in warm colors cover the sofa, chairs, and floor in the living room. The sofa is upholstered in green velvet, and the rug on the floor is in a solid color. Here and there, a romantic 19th-century touch is to be seen, such as the use of an India print on the large armchair. At the left of the fireplace a hollowed tree trunk—a more modern form of romanticism—holds pokers and tongs.

◀ In the big room, 19th-century furniture dominates: antique cross-back Louis Philippe armchairs, a Second Empire slipper chair near the first window, and a big "Voltaire" armchair of the same period further down the room. The colors here are warm, yet soft. The curtains are yellow felt, and the floor is red tile.

This unusual hallway under the eaves has a bright color scheme consisting of red ▶
wall-to-wall carpeting, green chairs, and brown and white wallpaper.

The long, low house seems to hug the site. The driveway meanders until it finally ends at the carport. Materials are used so as to achieve a contrast in textures: a painted wall, a chimney of dressed stone, and a long wall of stained wood.

AN ARCHITECT'S MODERN HOUSE
The home of Claude Richard

The house that Claude Richard built for himself on the outskirts of Saint-Quentin proves once and for all that there are no grounds for the French myth that a modern house is not in keeping with a traditionally gracious way of life. It also proves that the basic notions of modern architecture have been acclimated to the point where the influences of the United States, Scandinavia, and Japan have now blended into a coherent style that can be applied to everything, down to the smallest piece of furniture. In this design a series of parallel horizontals is evident in the concrete slab over the pool, the narrow terrace in front of the house, the massive eave, and the bookshelves inside the house. The heavy slab over the pool is raised a few inches so that it seems to float, and this concept is repeated in the coffee table and stools in the living room. The relationship between indoors and outdoors has been planned so that the architecture and the landscaping are in complete harmony. The rigid geometry of the house and the pool are relieved by the folds of the curtains and the placing of shrubs and trees around the pool.

◀ The house and its adjoining pool both seem extremely simple in design, and Frank Lloyd Wright's dictum that materials should never be disguised has been respectfully followed. Elementary geometric shapes such as the simple concrete slab across the pool are unadorned.

The same simplicity is evident in the living room. The ▶ rectangle of the fireplace wall of roughened concrete is the focal point of the room, and the space over the fireplace is used occasionally as a movie screen. The polished top of the mahogany coffee table is also a rectangle, while the nearby cushion is a perfect square.

217

▲
A fireplace separates the living area from the dining room. The dining table — mahogany with black wrought-iron legs — is placed so that diners have a view either of the garden or of adjoining rooms.

◄ The children's bedroom was kept simple for practical reasons as well as to conform to the spirit of the rest of the house. The gray carpeting makes a comfortable floor to play on, and the large blackboard is ideal for drawing and homework. Shelves are used to store toys, and, in addition, there are chests fitted underneath the beds and therefore more space in the room for playing.

The Japanese influence is apparent in the low furniture, ► and especially in the cushions set directly on the floor. The same influence is seen in the play of textures: polished wood, shaggy rug, close-cropped rug, terrazzo flooring. A row of built-in lights over the bookshelves throws diffused light that reflects into the room.

THE PRESBYTERY OF ESCLAVELLES

The proximity of the village has influenced the design of the manor. The door pediment and the lines of the roof are a rustic adaptation of classic forms.

The traditional French garden is suggested by the twin topiary balls at the edge of the lawn. This expanse of grass is like a pasture belonging to the manor.

The wrought-iron banister in the stair hall is a Louis XIV masterpiece, and the Flemish tapestry and the stag head are in keeping with the stately setting.

Grandeur and simplicity combine in a Norman manor house

This Louis XIV house was built in 1712. It is not as grand as a château, yet it is quite different from a peasant's cottage, and, consequently, it presented quite a challenge to the decorator. However, M. and Mme. Minot have managed to achieve just the right combination of splendor and simplicity. Straightforward panelling outlined with restrained molding appears in both the living and dining rooms. The wrought-iron banister and the faded colors of the Flemish tapestry in the hall are seen against a pure white background. For her high-ceilinged bedroom, Mme. Minot chose furniture that was massive enough not to be overpowered by the beams overhead and yet sufficiently formal to suit the panelling and the antique Louis XIV windows with their many panes. In the other more rustic bedrooms, the furnishings are countrified in feeling, the decoration switching from provincial sophistication to provincial simplicity, with delightful results.

A blue palette was typical of the 18th century and was appropriate for this sitting room. From the sapphire blue of the carpeting and the velvet on the Louis XVI armchairs, the eye goes to the pale blue of the rose-covered chintz, and then to the evanescent blue of the 18th century panelling. But blue alone can be melancholy; the subtle shadings of the silk Oriental rugs give enough contrast to bring the whole room to life.

◄ Panelling created at one time by Jansen was painted an eggshell color, as were the beams of the dining-room. Colors that were too bright would jar in a dwelling this old. On the sand-colored carpet, the black and gold Regency chairs sparkle without being garish.

The owners wanted a degree of stateliness, and this is apparent in Mme. Minot's bedroom. The fluted columns of the four-poster bed harmonize with the vertical emphasis of the architecture and panelling. The furniture was chosen for its massive, sturdy qualities: a Louis XIII armchair in one window embrasure, a table of the same period in the other window, and a desk beneath a Dutch painting. The fabrics are in cheerful colors: solid cornflower blue for the easy chair and tester, and the same blue against a white background on the *toile de Jouy* print used for the curtains and the cover on the chaise longue. A particularly ingenious idea was the trompe l'œil of fake bookcases that conceals the cupboards.

▲
M. Minot's bedroom could exist only in the country, and it has the country's traditionally timeless quality. The old beams on the ceiling and sloping walls, the sturdy Norman bed, the wood floor, and the striped throw rugs combine to give this room its special charm.

◄ Even more countrified is the son's bedroom, with its antique tile floor, rush-seated armchair, and simple curtains. The room looks informal despite the 18th-century bed and the stone mantelpiece.

THE PRESBYTERY
OF ESCLAVELLES *continued*

The remodeling of this farm by Mme. Vernant is interesting—first, because it was a real farmhouse with a real thatch roof; second, because Mme. Vernant respected the age of the 200-year-old building while decorating it; and, third, because the restorations followed no rigid rules. The result shows how valuable modern conveniences can be neatly fitted into an old house. Very little had to be done to the charming exterior except to renew the straw thatch, which is the most effective thermal insulator there is. Inside, the house was very primitive, as one might expect in an 18th-century farm. Everything that could be saved was saved, such as the exposed beams in the master bedroom. Walls and ceilings that were too damaged were covered with pine boarding. The furniture in the house is as simple as the architecture.

The dining room combines old and new elements ▶ against a background of pine boarding and black and white tiles. The farm table and benches are ageless, the chest is Louis XV, and the round table pure fantasy.

An alcove lined with blue and white fabric makes a cozy corner in the master bedroom. This room is almost Spartan in its lack of clutter, but the orange-red walls make it cheerful. The heavy beams on the ceiling have been painted to make them less oppressive, but they still give character to the setting.
▼

Fantasy shows up again in the living room (below right). English leather pigs, copied after old milking stools, stand before the hearth on a Spanish straw rug. In the alcove there is a leopard-covered sofa.

AN 18TH-CENTURY THATCHED COTTAGE
Restored with a minimum of changes

A RESTORED HOUSE AND BARN

Two units remodeled to suit the owner's main interests

Michel Pignères is a decorator who loves antique furniture and the subtle harmonies of old wood and soft fabrics, and because of this he has made his reputation among those who admire elegant decoration. But he is also a man with an absorbing hobby: underwater fishing. He quite rightly realized that these two predilections could not be successfully combined in a single decorating scheme, so he applied schemes that were diametrically opposed in the two buildings on his property which is not far from Paris. In one, there is a coruscating brilliance, and everything catches the eye: bright colors, strange marine trophies, bold conceits. All this is contained in the single room of the remodeled barn. In the house itself, M. Pignères has created subtle harmonies and charming rooms, and although almost everything was restored, this was not apparent. The old house was a typical bourgeois residence with handsome mantelpieces, and they are still there. But on the outside, the walls were covered with roughened stucco, the terrace was paved with stones, and stained oak shutters were added to windows, which had been newly cut. Here, the short walk from one building to the other is a journey from one way of life — and consequently one kind of decoration — to another.

At first glance, the little barn lying a short distance from the house seemed useless. But M. Pignères "buried" it three feet by raising the grade outside, thus giving it better proportions. Then he removed the old door and cut a new window in front to make it look habitable.

Strange objects appear in this décor. The urn holds dried plants and odd bits of driftwood. Above the Spanish lowboy are stuffed fish heads, sawfish bills, a turtle shell, and the gaping jaws of a ◀ shark.

Many elements were used to give new life to M. Pignères' bedroom. The old exposed beams were replaced by new ones. The Louis XV mantelpiece was given better proportions by reducing its apparent height with a raised hearth. New windows with many small lights in the 18th-century manner were installed throughout the house. No rigid adherence to a single style was intended. The Hungarian-point rugs by Deheselle and the 19th-century chairs harmonize with the 18th-century elements and the Clayette lithograph.

1

A RESTORED
HOUSE AND BARN *continued*

1. Like the barn, the house was also too high for its size, so the land was graded and 31 inches of the house were buried. The floors were raised, and the doors were enlarged and new windows cut through the walls. 2. The attic floor was removed to give greater height to the ground-floor rooms. 3. An open wooden staircase was built and the bottom was covered by planks lined with chintz to give a greater feeling of security. 4. On the balcony, metal strips support shelves covered in the same fabric as the walls. 5. A Renaissance mantel adds an imposing touch. 6. In the kitchen, the use of Italian mosaic and turquoise floor tiles makes it clear that no fake farmhouse kitchen was attempted. However, the varnished oak and the wrought-iron knobs and hinges are in keeping with the country setting. (Opposite) Contrasting colors and textures make a perfect background for the unusual collection of objects M. Pignères has assembled. Turtle shells and fish bills make a dramatic display against the bare stone wall.

2

3

4

5

6

1

2

3

The farm of Maillebois presented a formidable remodeling job, the kind that required reinforcements and certain additions to the original structure without changing the outward appearance. Mr. Lageson, the young American who bought this farm, and Mr. Eller, a painter to whom he entrusted the remodeling, were too enchanted by the countryside, the architecture, and the character of Normandy to make any radical changes. On the other hand, they were too accustomed to modern conveniences to be willing to give up any of these luxuries. The roof was repaired and kept in its original shape. The half-timbered walls and the dormer window were carefully preserved, but the wooden shutter was replaced by a many-paned casement window. Opposite the front gate, the wagon shed was transformed into a living room by the addition of a window wall. The interior of the barn is the most striking example of how well the remodeling plan succeeded, for here new partitions had to be added without damaging the original timbers. The ceiling beams were reinforced where it was absolutely necessary.

Throughout most of the house provincial furniture has been used to give the house an air of comfort. But not all of it is rustic — as witness the Napoleon III mahogany chairs.

A NORMAN FARM
A remodeled one-story house near Dreux

1. Furnishing an odd corner can become quite an art: at one end of this living room, a small desk stands out against the white walls and somber wood beams. 2. The living room door, big as a barn door, lets sunlight flood into the room. The terra-cotta tile floor (in a toast color) is in the best country tradition. 3. The beams of the old wagon shed were not changed, nor was the lath work, which had never been plastered over. 4. The dark walls carry the eye to the fireplace, which is surrounded by rough white plaster. 5. In order to keep the feeling of space, hardly any break was planned between the living room and the front hall. The huge stone that makes a partial divider between the hall and the dining area was an old watering trough. The opening in the stone wall eads to the adjoining kitchen.

1

1. The breakfast corner in the kitchen has a background of pure Norman half-timbering. 2 and 3. On the outside, the façades were carefully preserved. The gaping opening of the barn was fitted with windows divided by strong vertical muntins to match the half-timbered walls. 4. Seen from the newly created garden, the house still shows its true rustic character.

THE ART OF REMODELING SMALL SPACES

5, 6, and 7. A taste for barns inspires our holiday dreams. The master bedroom under the eaves was remodeled with this in mind. The fireplace that had to be installed is typically rustic: the hearth is two steps up, the sides are brick, the lintel is a wooden beam supported by two stones. A small hood of rough white plaster adds a simple, archaic touch without belonging to any particular era.

THE STORY OF A MILL
Neglected through the centuries

On the banks of the Loing at Châtillon-Coligny, only about an hour's drive from Paris, the mill of the Montmorency-Luxembourgs retains its 17th-century look.

This was a romantic mill, filled with mementos of the Montmorency-Luxembourgs who had it built around 1675. It is still romantic, but it is no longer a mill. Because of the ingenious remodeling by M. and Mme. Dechamboux, few changes can be seen from the outside. One that is apparent is the long, flattish dormer windows that let daylight into the bedrooms under the eaves. Here and there are other indications that windows have been enlarged to make the building more habitable. But the mossy paving stones in the courtyard and the ivy that grows on the turret suggest that nothing has been disturbed. Inside, the same respect has been paid to the past, and in one instance, an omission was rectified: the dining-room floor was paved in stone following a typical pattern found in 17th-century manors. Modern conveniences have been so skillfully concealed that one is hardly conscious of them. An oil heater warms the house, and the roof has been insulated with polystyrene foam — both important points for a house in a humid location. For the furnishings, M. and Mme. Dechamboux decided on the simple, straightforward Louis XIII style as best suited to country living and to the rugged architecture of the mill itself.

◀ A gallery (far left, opposite)—unusual in a 17th-century house—runs around the entire front hall and offsets its excessive height, but its oak joists and balustrade do not clash with the simple country architecture. The faded greenery of the 17th-century tapestry and the vase of flowers are the only notes of color. A copy of an old oak table and a 17th-century chair from Lorraine have the appropriate sturdy dignity, and the bare, monastic quality of the flagstone floor is in keeping. Double glass doors have been fitted into the arched opening.

A large provincial sideboard and a farm dining table have the right country look. The subject of the 18th-century cartoon for a tapestry is very appropriate in this former millhouse, since it is now often used as a hunting lodge during the season.

◀ In country houses, the cozy charm of an open fire calls for large mantelpieces of stone and wood. The arrangement of the Louis XIII armchairs and the sofa around the fireplace is an English idea that has been popular for some time in France both for formal decorating schemes and for hunting lodges. Here the tradition has even been carried to the point of placing a Louis XIII table at the back of the sofa. The geometric pattern of the floor laid by Berger of Argent-sur-Sauldre is traditional. The light blue walls and the curtains of yellow mattress ticking are more modern.

▲
There are almost no passages, but changes of level help to separate one room from the next. The use of short jogs of wall at either side of this flight of steps is a very free adaptation of a 17th-century concept. The same is true of the solid wood bookcase.

◀ A unique case frames the radiator and also holds a collection of books and bibelots. Both the risers and the shelves were made of natural oak to match the rest of the furniture in the decorative scheme planned around textures of wood and stone. Even the window has a wooden sill and dado, and wooden planks outline the lozenge-design tile floor that is typical of the Louis XVIII period.

THE STORY OF A MILL *continued*

▲
What looks like an old, ivy-covered turret was actually built quite recently.

▲
The flowing water of the Loing, which runs softly between gently sloping, grassy banks, is one of the principal charms of the mill. The character of the building has not been altered by the creation of a formal garden, which would have been completely out of place in this authentically rural setting.

Imagination was given free rein in the guest rooms. ▶
Here, the dormer window is dressed in a garlanded fabric, a style that was popular in old-fashioned provincial town houses. The same fresh, simple quality characterizes the large brass 19th-century bed, the Napoleon III slipper chair, and the delicate shaving stand.

A MODERN PAINTER REMODELS A FARM
A combination of antiquity, rusticity, and modernity

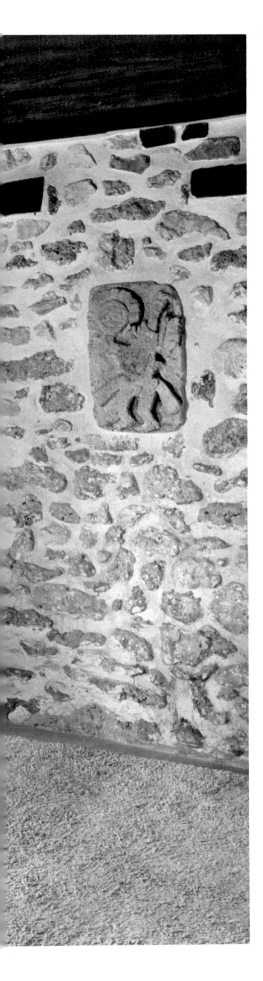

When they bought an old, run-down farmhouse and barn near Montfort-l'Amaury, M. and Mme. Van Leyden did not take long to decide which building should become the main house. They agreed that both should be, and they joined the two buildings together. On the exterior they made use of the very old, traditional combination of mortared ashlar and weathered tiles. New dormer windows were cut into the roof. A long, sloping shape was chosen to make the least possible change in the roof line, and many-paned windows in the 18th-century style were used. Inside the house, the passage of time had caused considerable havoc, but whatever old timbers were still sound were saved. Apart from these details, the owners were largely inspired by modern American architecture. Raised fireplaces have the look of antiquity, owing to the use of arches, but they are really a modern concept. A storage cabinet and a snack-bar are all that separate the dining room and the kitchen—an arrangement that would not look out of place in Connecticut. Throughout the house, a collection of European and American folk art adds a note of fantasy to the decoration.

◄ Bare ashlar walls inside the house are a modern concept. They make the best possible background for a 17th-century bas relief, the kind of object that is very difficult to place elsewhere. The monastic austerity of the decoration—which is not lessened by the shaggy white rug on the stone floor—makes a perfect setting for a collection of pre-Columbian terra cottas.

The old barn was extended to join the ► farmhouse. The extension narrows to fit the two old buildings, and its irregularity has all the charm of additions made through the centuries.

A MODERN PAINTER REMODELS A FARM *continued*

▲ A snack-bar separates the kitchen from the dining room. This is an entirely modern arrangement — as modern as the kitchen appliances — but it does not clash with the 100-year-old architecture because of the materials that were chosen: wood, brick, and whitewashed walls, all of which are in the traditional peasant manner.

◄ A cabinet-divider hides the actual work area of the kitchen. It is deep enough to leave room for the niche that holds a primitive giraffe. The simplicity of the design of the snack bar allows it to blend unobtrusively into the decoration.

Since the owner is a painter, he ► has provided the principal color with one of his large collages, which hangs by the fireplace. It is unframed, and this suits the peasant décor and also fits in with the modern trend toward less ornamentation. The dining-table top is a heavy plank over six feet long, and the many-branched candelabrum on the table is a modern creation made from salvaged oil cans. The leopard and the stools are primitive carvings.

FARMHOUSE NEAR BRINON

Hidden virtues have been brought to light

What was simply an old house now looks like a charming antique, and it was accomplished not by creating anything new but simply by enhancing what already existed. The roof line was modified, new dormer windows were added, and the electric power mast was removed. Much of the effect was also due to the right choice of materials.

The country attic has kept its simplicity. The exposed beams are its principal charm, and here they are used as a background on which to hang prints and mementos of World War I. A single style of furniture would be pointless in such a setting. The armchair in front of the late-19th-century mahogany desk is Régence, the other armchairs are Empire, the console table is Louis XVI, and the low chest is a country design in natural wood.

The 18th-century charm of the large room on the ground floor was achieved by quite simple means. The proportions are, of course, an important factor, as are the sturdy beams and the terrazzo floor. The portraits make a gallery of ancestors against the white, rough-plaster walls. The mahogany table and the Louis XVI sideboard are in keeping with the décor of an old manor.

Although it possessed a basic unity, this small farmhouse near Brinon lacked character. In this respect it was like thousands of other similar structures in the Ile-de-France dating from one of the less glorious moments of the 19th century when Louis Philippe was on the throne. But now, since its transformation, it is quite hard even to find the outlines of the original structure. In actual fact, the changes were not as drastic as they may seem. The eaves were extended slightly, and the barely perceptible curve combines with the weathered tiles to make the roof look centuries old. A half-timbered veneer gives the façade character, and the additional windows add to the apparent length of the house. Inside, the job was more simple. The oak beams were exposed and the ceiling between them painted white. The floors were surfaced with pink Italian marble terrazzo, which gives the rooms an unsuspected dignity. The owner's wife, with the help of local artisans and suppliers, decorated the rooms simply and tastefully. The attic already existed, but it was made more habitable by adding larger dormer windows and putting in a parquet floor.

Eclecticism is the rule in the guest rooms. The 19th-century bed is Portuguese; the 17th-century waxed oak chair comes from Lorraine.

A unique feature is the door-bookcase made to look like the door of a Louis XIV armoire. The narrow shelves hold a collection of books in old bindings. ▲

RECONSTRUCTION OF A LOUIS XIV BARN
A rural delight in the Vexin

Barns can have many virtues, and when they are constructed with handsome timbers dating back to the days of Louis XIV they are masterpieces that deserve to be saved. This occured to Dr. and Mme. Roucaute, two Parisians who were looking for a place in the country, when they discovered the virtual ruins of this 17th-century structure near Gisors, surrounded by a field, woods, and a trout stream. It took them three years of work to make the three-hundred-year-old barn habitable. The old floor of beaten earth was rebuilt and covered with red tiles. Windows and glass doors were let into the walls. In one wing—the highest part of the old barn—a gallery looks down on the new living room. In the other wing, the guest rooms and the low-ceilinged proportions are more typical of country houses. But the total effect is a rural delight.

Styles from the Renaissance to Louis XV, from the Auvergne to Normandy, have been most tastefully mixed in the great living room. The panels of a 16th-century altarpiece hang over a modern copy of a Louis XV sofa. Over a carved cherrywood mantelpiece, brought from a house in the Aveyron, musical instruments are hung in the manner of the Renaissance. The Majorcan straw rugs are modern, as is the ironwork chandelier designed by the owner and forged by a local craftsman.

◄ Seen from the gallery, the living room looks like a romantic stage set. The gallery itself acts as a study and as a guest room when additional sleeping space is needed.

Suggestions for a new country style

The indoor garden is the oddest element of the game room. The concrete floor stops at the edge of an area covered with sand. On the mantelpiece is a famous oil by Drian.

◀ An unusual mixture of traditional country styles, overstuffed furniture that goes back to before World War II, and a few fashionable modern touches give the living room its informal quality. The painted beam that holds the flowerpots is a free interpretation of a Scandinavian idea. Drian's easel holds his self-portrait and his palette. With the exception of the table, which dates from the end of the Louis XIV era, the furniture is really of no particular style—simply comfortable, practical pieces that are common in the French provinces and suited to country living.

▼

This is not a farmhouse but a modest peasant's cottage. The painter Drian and, after him, an old friend who took over the house, have been careful not to change its essential character. In fact, the major work that had to be done has tended to emphasize it. In the living room, a terra-cotta tile floor was put in which goes well with the white walls and old, scarred beams—originally part of the stable. In the adjoining room, now a game room, the rough plaster walls are typical of country wagon sheds. Against this background, the influence of modern art is felt throughout the house. An indoor sanded garden occupies one corner of the game room at a slightly lower level than the floor. The mantelpiece and walls here have a consciously roughened texture. The result is unique and perhaps heralds a new country style somewhere between the traditionally rustic and the modern decoration imported from the city.

A stronger feeling for tradition distinguishes the bedroom décor. The bed and the side table are Empire, the provincial armoire is 19th-century in the Louis XV style but with Louis XVI fluting and a Louis Philippe cornice at the top.

Fitted into the mountainside, the chalet has the irregular shape that has been traditional from time immemorial. An exterior staircase leads up to a balcony and to the main rooms. The exterior siding is wooden planking, a traditional material that acts as a good insulator.

A MOUTAIN RETREAT

An architect's chalet in Savoy

A beautiful mountain site inspired architects Bernard Baudouin and Pierre Peltier to create a style around wood and stone. The timbers are in peasant tradition, as are the white-painted walls, but the crazy-paving slate flooring is a new idea in a region where the natives never have stone floors. The fireplace, a raised hearth built onto an angle of the room, owes its conception to contemporary American architecture. The furniture clearly shows the taste for simplicity that is becoming more and more popular, but it is an understated simplicity and carefully avoids any "picturesque" characteristics. The fruitwood table is in a style inherited from the 19th century, and the rough-hewn rush-seated chairs are modern copies of a style that is more or less dateless.

◀ The same shades are used on the glass door and on the window. They let in plenty of light but diffuse the blinding reflection of sun from the snowy slopes.

◀ The eaves slope down right over the balcony and beyond for protection against snowstorms. The balcony itself follows the two sides of the house that face the view of the valley below.

The rough surface of the slate floor goes ▶ well with the natural wood of the chairs and the joists. Bark was left on the central beam to give the room the rustic feeling of a cabin on the mountainside. The fireplace is modern.

The decoration created in a chalet at Gstaad by Paul Bourquin, a disciple of André Arbus, may herald the revival of regional styles. What this Swiss architect and decorator undertook for Mme. Antoinette Notz is not an exact copy but an adaptation of a traditional chalet interior. In building the house, he used ancient construction methods. In the living and dining rooms, the walls are of rough-cast plaster mixed with sand that was given a special rubbing treatment to achieve a pleasant antique look. Throughout the house urban furnishings, such as the overstuffed sofas and the shaggy rug, are mixed with simple furniture made from the wood of the Canton of Valais. Even though the chalet is actually in the Bernese Oberland, it is on the border of the Valais. Traditional details appear alongside ideas borrowed from modern architecture, such as the brick that angles one corner of the dining room and the blend of rough plaster walls and knotty pine panelling in the living room. The result is a unique mixture of modern taste and a vigorous local style.

LOCAL STYLES
Based on peasant traditions

The living room, with its view of the mountains, is a mixture of traditional chalet decoration and modern architecture. The face-to-face sofas are covered with the same gold and gray fabric used for curtains.

Peasant furniture always looks good against plain ▶ white walls. This rustic background gives full effect to the quality of natural wood of the milking stools, the 18th-century sideboard from the Valais, and the farm table in the middle of the room. The panelled wood ceiling adds character to the room.

An antique armoire from the Valais was cut apart to create this bedroom wall. The center alcove holds a sofa, and the niches at either side are fitted with bookshelves. The walls are covered with a printed cotton by Pierre Frey that has a fresh peasant quality. A similar niche at the other end of this room shelters the bed. ▼

In the evening, the hooded fireplace in the living room becomes the center of attraction. The two sofas are placed facing each other and at right angles to the fireplace, following the English custom that is now popular all over the Continent. A rustic coffee table stands in between. ▼

A corner banquette in the kitchen marks off the breakfast area. The supports for the banquette were carved to complement the early-19th-century table from the Valais. A narrow shelf back of the banquette serves to display a collection of pewter. On the wall are butter molds and old churns. ▼

SMALL PARIS APARTMENTS

At the top of the stairs.

Sometimes, at the end of those staircases that seem to go spiraling upward forever, one finds an attic or a small room with a wonderful view of Paris and a charm due to its cozy proportions. This sort of room is best decorated in a friendly and unpretentious manner, with wit and plenty of imagination. On these pages are a few of the fascinating creations that have evolved under the rooftops of Paris.

A taste for unusual symbols is evident in Katia Grotkamp's paintings and decorating. The bat is the talisman of the Austrian side of her family, the other half of which is Russian. The walls are used as a display area for her paintings, most of them hung without frames. An 18th-century Russian samovar sparkles against the cool white of the walls.

Brass, old wood, and sumptuous fabrics are blended in rustic harmony. Here and there, unexpected details stand out sharply and reflect the painter's taste. A rope ladder and an old chain that once supported a scale hang from the rafters. Lightly hung Japanese net floats and a stunning zebra skin, whose stripes assume fantastic proportions in the restricted space, give the décor character.

A loft in Montparnasse
A PAINTER'S STUDIO APARTMENT

In decorating, adventures can occur in all sorts of odd corners — and sometimes even under the plaster of a wall. When the painter Katia Grotkamp dreamed, as all painters do, of finding just the right studio, and finally settled for two small adjoining rooms with an even smaller compartment containing a sink, she thought that she had acquired the most ordinary apartment in the world. At best, it was tucked quietly away from the clatter of the city, down at the end of a small courtyard. To make it more serviceable, after consulting an architect she had the partition between the rooms pulled down. The marvelous surprise was that she found she had uncovered the fine old supporting timbers seen in this photograph. The timbers suggested the existence of a beamed ceiling, and in a few days this too was uncovered. The result was that a two-room apartment with a kitchen became a barn-like loft right in the middle of Paris. The cleaned and waxed timbers set the tone for the decoration: off-white for the ceiling between the beams ; massive, sturdy furniture (some of the pieces are rare Austrian and Russian antiques) ; and unusual objects here and there. The paintings covering the walls are almost exclusively Katia's own works, and these also allow the mind and eye to wander beyond the ordinary confines of the room.

◄ The apartment is at the far end of a little courtyard near Montparnasse.

◀ Since the apartment is both a studio and a home, the eminently functional easel also serves as a screen to shield the front door. Jars of pigments are lined up on the beam over the cupboard, which is a family piece dating from 1787. It helps to give the entire apartment the feeling of an ancestral home.

The vibrant rhythm of a Proven- ▶ çal bead curtain makes a visual separation between the studio and the kitchen, and a black sliding door can be closed to shut off the kitchen entirely. Since the ceiling of the kitchen is lower than the ceiling in the rest of the apartment, a storage space was provided between the two.

◀ Family heirlooms have been set on this carved chest, dated 1752, in an almost haphazard fashion. The bulging samovar and the other brass pieces are mementos of the Austrian Empire and Russia.

The kitchen and the bathroom ▶ seen via the pass-through that opens on to the studio. Architect Jean Garet planned both these rooms. The double sink and stove are on the left in the kitchen, and the refrigerator is tucked under the pass-through. The bathroom was fitted into a small compartment and contains a washbasin, hip-bath, and other accessories. Everything is painted pale green, accented by black "Céralux" on the walls.

AUSTRIAN AND RUSSIAN HEIRLOOMS

To give a feeling of ▶ length to a very short entrance hall, white thermoplastic tiles were laid here and in the living room beyond. The double row of 19th-century prints and the radiator shelf, which extends the full length of the hall, lead the eye into the distance. The cornflower blue rug unrolls like a ceremonial carpet and also leads the eye onward.

MODERN DECOR NEAR LES INVALIDES
Modern art under the eaves.

The surprise begins right at the bottom of the stairs. To reach this apartment perched on the top floor of a house facing Les Invalides, it is necessary to climb an open metal staircase fastened to the outside of the house. At the top of the stairs the front door opens on three small steps that lead down into a miniature front hall which in turn leads to two rooms. The front hall has a half Charles X, half English air, which results from the varied collection of 19th-century prints. There is little hint of a modern-looking apartment until one reaches the living room and bedroom. This unexpected change appears not only in the abstract paintings by Fautrier, Poliakoff, and others, but also in the interplay of colors among the pictures. Yet the details in the rooms show great restraint. There are none of the strident qualities so often found in modern decoration. A comfortable 19th-century easy chair has been included, as though it were a valuable antique. The final surprise is the bathroom, tucked in between the rooms, behind white curtains, with its tub sheathed in mahogany.

No inch of space ▶ is wasted. In a corner of the living room, an angled Directoire table fits neatly and holds a black bronze model of the Vendôme column. The slope of the mansard roof did not deter the owner from hanging a Segonzac etching.

◄ The problem of how to hang curtains in the dormer windows of a mansard roof is ingeniously solved here. The top of the window embrasure is covered with midnight blue moire, and the same fabric is used for the fixed curtains. In this way, the depth of the embrasure, rather than the slope of the walls, is emphasized. White muslin undercurtains bordered with blue braid can be drawn across the windows. The easy chair covered in yellow Chinese silk contrasts boldly with the blue curtains. The mirror, set in a shallow niche, makes the room seem almost twice its length.

Each side of the living room has a distinct personality. The door from the front hall has been made almost invisible by painting it the same dark gray color as the two adjoining walls. A simple white molding outlines the built-in bookshelves which balance the bedroom door (not shown). Over the wrought-iron console table is a turquoise blue painting by Paniaras. To the right are paintings by Atlan, Zai Wou-ki, and Matta. The comfortable armchair is in leather and the columnar lamp, bought in Italy, is of white tole. ▼

A CRISP AND LIVELY DECORATING SCHEME

A gamut of blues — dark gray with a touch of blue on the walls, the dull blue of the large carpet, blues of every shade in the modern paintings — give the living room a surprising freshness. The greige canvas of the sofa, the white mats on several of the pictures, and the white panel framing the mirror emphasize the room's brilliance. Without molding or cornices, the walls make an admirablebackground for the pictures: above the sofa a Fautrier, then a Poliakoff and a Max Ernst; on the rear wall, a Dubuffet with a Fautrier gouache over it; near the jog another Fautrier, and under it a Sam Pappas lit from below by the lamp.

Between the bedroom and the living-room, the bathroom has the air of a boudoir where old and new make a curious mixture. New: the gamut of contrasting colors. Old: the idea of a bathtub fitted into a curtained alcove and encased in mahogany to match the washstand with its white and gold basin and its two gold faucets.

The first thing that strikes one in this house that dates back to the 1860s is the feeling of spaciousness. To achieve this, Mme. Goldsmith removed the doors that previously separated the living and dining rooms. All that remains of this division is a single pillar, which is structurally necessary and conveniently creates the effect of a portico. The feeling of space and unity is further enhanced by the continuous parquet flooring and by the use of the same kind of furniture — black wrought-iron garden furniture and candelabra with simple lines. Mme. Goldsmith has used parallel lines and perspectives everywhere. The parallels show up in the stripes of the mattress ticking that covers the furniture and hangs as window curtains and portières. The perspectives are counterbalanced by imaginary ones in the mirrored wall of the dining area. The color scheme is largely black and white against a greige background, which makes a restful and airy combination. No gilt or shiny surfaces are to be seen, and no little bibelots or small-scaled furniture clutter the rooms. The only ornaments here are green potted plants and the wall decorations, which are either geometric designs in brick or abstract panels or pure black. Abstract is indeed the key word here. The owner has successfully transformed the lessons of Mondrian and Poliakoff into decorating, even to the use of black and white.

In the rue des Ursins, off the quai des Fleurs, little remains from the distant past except the old vaulted cellars. The upper floors have the provincial charm of the beginning of the Second Empire.

ABSTRACT DESIGN
A modern apartment
with space and style

◀ Half front hall, half dining room, the ▶ room next to the living room has one entire wall of mirror that makes it seem much larger than it actually is. The choice of colors adds to the effect. The pale blue ceilings of both rooms rest on white cornices and thus appear higher. At mealtime, the garden table that stands along one wall is brought out and set at right angles to the mirror so that every diner can share the delightful feeling of spaciousness.

A stunning — but not blinding — clarity distinguishes Mme Goldsmith's black and white kitchen. The refrigerator, walls, stove and mixer are all enameled black. On the right-hand wall, but not seen in the photo, are three panels of sharp blue, black and olive green. The concrete floor is covered with a smooth white plastic paint.

The light colors of the living room are the most remarkable characteristic. The brick ▶ wall has been given an ocher tint that recalls the Place des Vosges. The two sofas that boldly occupy the center of the room have an air of lightness thanks to their mattress-ticking upholstery. The long coffee table — an antique stone mantelpiece — accentuates the parallel stripes on the furniture, the window-seat cushions and on the roll-up window blinds all made of the same material.

2

A ROMANTIC ATTIC
With timbers and panelling

The ups and downs of life have their own special charms, particularly in an attic. Instead of trying to make a set of conventional rooms out of this studio apartment right under the sloping roof, decorator France Bertin first of all created a large living room with different levels. The barnlike effect was enhanced when the old, low ceiling was removed to reveal antique beams. These were treated so that a fine patina was achieved. Despite the rustic background, the lower floor (1) has a romantic softness, created through the use of old gold wall-to-wall carpeting and the natural oak panelling. In this unusual setting, the ladder to the upper level, where a baldaquin over the bed can just be seen, does not seem out of place. The same can be said for the sculptures by Guy Lartigue: the owl on the small round table and the tortoise at the foot of the ladder. In contrast to the height of the living room, the original ceiling was kept in the studio area. In the long, low sitting room (2), the walls were covered with old gold shantung to match the carpeting, and the furniture was cleverly arranged to fit under the eaves. A gray woolen fabric brightened with old gold *passementerie* was used to upholster the furniture and for the curtains ; the fabric serves to soften the décor and gives a cozy feeling to the room. The doors were painted in two shades of gray heightened by ocher moldings, and the baseboards were marbleized in a deep blue-gray. The Empire armchairs and the 19th-century mahogany desk are simple enough to fit the setting. Except for the small bathroom (3) with its polished mahogany walls, like an old coffer, everything in the décor has the easy, relaxed air of a peaceful retreat.

Like a stage set, the apartment reveals hidden corners and unsuspected uses. The living room is on the lower level, and the bedroom is above, under the skylights.

In some parts of the apartment, the old ceiling was retained. The sitting room stretches out in a long, narrow shape, lined with prints and 19th-century furniture.

The miniature bathroom evokes the romantic feeling of the apartment.

3

◀ It would be hard to classify this ▶ as a dining room, a study, or a second living room, and in fact it is used as all three, depending on the occasion. The monastery table doubles as an excellent work table. This is set next to the kitchen, seen just beyond the portière of Egyptian fabric. To the left (not shown) is the adjacent living room. The niches seem like additional doorways and openings, and they demonstrate the rule that the more openings a room has, the more spacious it seems.

The cheerful abstract sun, painted on the door by a friend of the owners.

IN THE HEART OF OLD PARIS
A touch of the country

In Olivier and Varenka Marc's apartment, an offbeat note is immediately struck by the front door, which is covered with a flush panel of plywood rubbed down with white lead on which a grinning sunburst is painted. It is difficult to realize that the apartment is in the heart of old Paris — on the Ile-St-Louis. The space was originally taken up by two tiny badly arranged apartments without kitchen, but all traces of the former state have disappeared. Here one forgets the typical atmosphere of the neighborhood and the characteristic solemnity of the Louis XIV houses nearby. There is a feeling of freshness and modernity. In the study-dining room, the country is suggested by the bare white walls, monastery table, rush-seated chairs, and the red portière that pulls back to reveal the kitchen. In the living room, abstract art in the avant-garde manner is featured. It is hard to tell whether the fireplace owes its inspiration to Arp and Brancusi or to typical Mediterranean cottages. Throughout the apartment, ingenious ideas abound, yet all of them seem quite in place. For example, the storage wall built between the dining room and the kitchen hides radiators and pipes, and its niches serve as display cases. Another example is the use of the old beams as decorative elements. They were found under layers of wallpaper, and although it was a stroke of luck to have come across them, good decoration depends on making the most of such lucky finds.

MINIMUM SPACE ON THE ILE ST-LOUIS

▲
An exotic air that is universal in appeal yet predominantly Mediterranean inspired the decoration in the living room, and all the objects are mementos of the owners' trips. Between the windows with their curtains from the Cyclades are a Japanese chest and a tapestry woven by children in the studio of the Egyptian architect Ouissa Wassef.

The sculptured fireplace gives this corner an air of fantasy, despite the fact that everything ▶ is simplicity itself. A sprightly rooster, an owl, and gourds highlight a décor that is simultaneously bare and upholstered. An area rug is spread over the wall-to-wall carpeting, and the sofa is covered with fur.

The beams, uncovered beneath layers of old wallpaper, contribute to the semi-abstract effect of the arrangement at one end of the room. Against the white wall, the colorful Coptic and Poirier tapestries stand out clearly and resemble the layout of a page in a book on modern art.
▼
In this corner, the high wooden bookcases have a bottom row of cabinets decorated with Varenka Marc's floral compositions.
▼

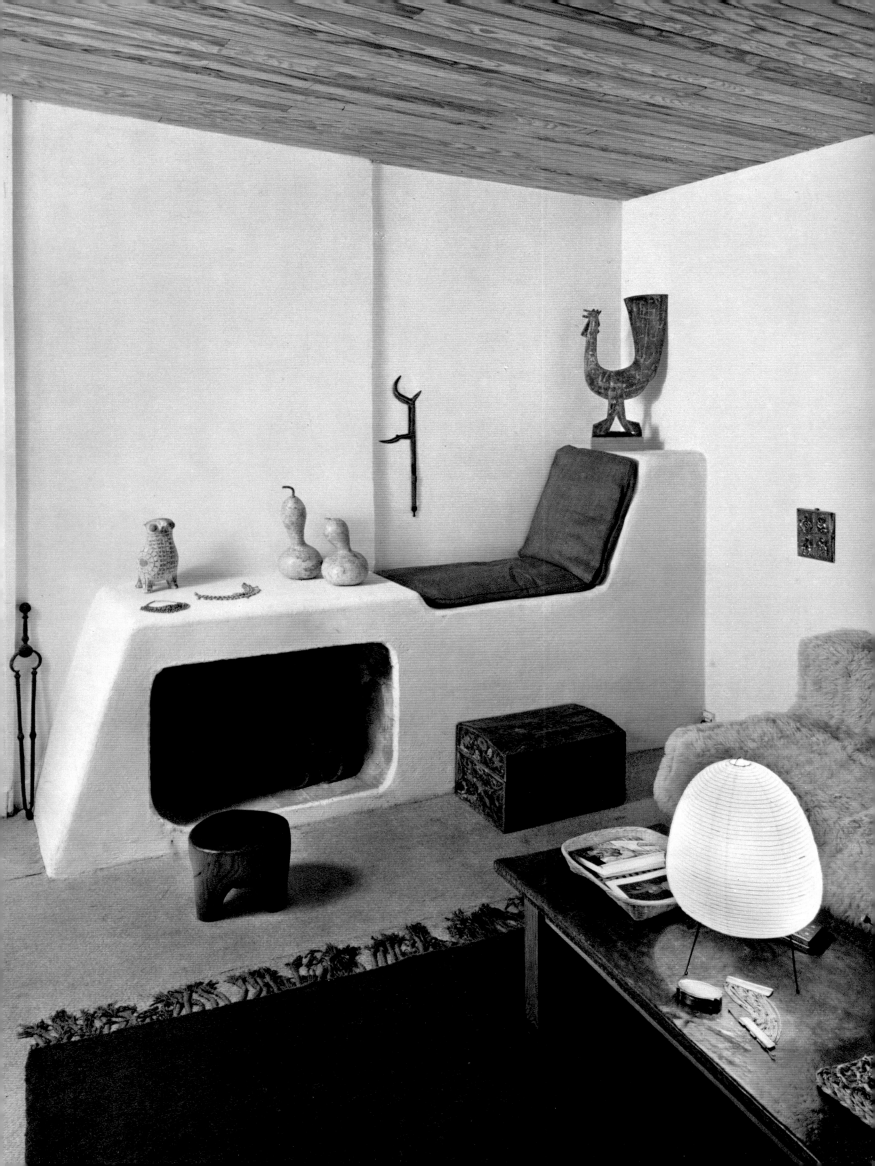

TWO ROOMS MADE INTO ONE

A witty and functional apartment

Comfortable living areas were made out of two servants' quarters on the top floor of the old town house of General de Mac-Mahon near the Hotel des Invalides. In converting these rooms into an apartment, the writer Gordon Merrick combined two themes: the simplest elements from the 19th century and the graceful lightness of modern design. In one corner a serpentine sofa hides a radiator. At the other end of the room a metal spiral staircase was installed that takes up much less space than conventional stairs. This leads to a garden on a terrace. A practical and, at the same time, witty device, is the sliding door that opens in the middle of the huge map of Paris and leads to the kitchen.

▲
To conceal the radiator, a curving sofa was chosen. In front of this is a coffee table made out of a Louis XVI table with its legs cut down. A side chair, two armchairs, and an old oil lamp wired for electricity complete the decoration.

A disturbing impression of fragility that ▶ is totally unfounded makes this metal staircase an amusing element in the decoration. Instead of free-standing bookcases, built-in shelves line all the walls and extend over the hall door that leads to the dining room and kitchen.

A screen divides the study area from the rest of the living room, and two armchairs carefully placed back to back emphasize the division between the two areas.

Visible from the living room, is the vast map of Paris, dated 1734, in the dining room. The sheets, which have not aged uniformly, were cut from an 18th-century book and pasted side by side on the wall. They completely hide the sliding door that leads to the kitchen. ▶

IN THE "MEZZANINES" OF THE REGENT
Conformity gets short shrift

▲
The view down to the garden of the Palais-Royal was the main attraction of the living room. The white curtains, bordered in black, are held in place with turquoise-blue tiebacks. They are almost a parody of a stage set, but they make the windows look higher than they actually are and almost hide the arches. In addition, the continuous material gives a feeling of lightness to the entire wall. A low black screen hides a radiator. An uninteresting table is hidden under a velvet covering in a manner typical of the 17th century.

M. Rico Zermeno, the art director of an advertising agency, held two trump cards when he decorated his apartment in the Palais-Royal. He had made a lucky discovery of the "mezzanines" in the old residence of the Duc d'Orléans, and with his professional training he had the necessary creative ideas to make this apartment original. Certainly no established rules could be followed in an apartment where the windows were the tops of arches surrounding the garden and where the general proportions were quite outside any of the accepted canons. M. Zermeno made a vast stage set out of the glass wall, partly hiding it behind white curtains trimmed with black. He divided up the living room into a study area around the desk and a conversation area around the sofa, without paying attention to the usual rules of furniture arrangement. He has put old prints and bibelots all over the place — most of them bought for very little. There is nothing classic about the way they are displayed, for tradition is respected, but in a modern manner.

Everywhere, M. Zermeno has broken ▶ decorating rules, but he has done this with taste. He has hung pictures of various schools, combining them with reproductions and a Greek bas-relief. The four legs of an old garden bench were turned upside down and covered with a marble slab to make a coffee table. The piece of furniture at the left was designed by the owner to house his hi-fi equipment and also to serve as one arm of the sofa. The base of the sofa is covered with marbleized paper to match the top of the coffee table.

◀ A passage underneath the living room leads out to the rue Montpensier. In this view, the pictures over the sofa are visible.

Toward the bedroom (below left) there is a change in the color scheme but no change in style. The bedroom curtains echo the chestnut brown and dark chocolate tones of the sofa. At this end of the living room, modern and traditional pieces are mixed. The brilliant reds of the painting by Fred Jessup surmount an Empire mahogany chest decorated with gilt bronze.

The details in the living room are also unorthodox. The desk lamp was a 19th-century oil lamp for which the owner found a chimney and a translucent globe. Two wall brackets of gilded gesso, made by an artist friend, support carved wooden Medici urns filled with dried flowers — something one expects to see on a table rather than high on a wall.

▼

UNDER THE EAVES
The charm of a real mansard roof

▲
A handsome double door in the panelling reveals not a vista of further rooms but a convenient, comfortable folding bed.

Every nook is put to good use. Here, where ▶ there is no headroom, a desk fills the wall space and is completely usable.

The honey tones of the living room (opposite) look even more golden in contrast to the blue-green of the wall-to-wall carpeting.

At the top of a house in the Place Vendôme, right under a mansard roof designed by Mansard himself, decorator Maurice Chalom transformed a couple of servants' rooms into a Parisian pied-à-terre for a New York businessman. With most of the original walls torn down, the spacious room allows for easy entertaining. The handsome wooden Georgian mantel came from England and set a theme that was carried out with pine panelling decorated with carved moldings. The panelling, in turn, made it very simple to hide a bed in the wall. On either side of the alcove that holds the bed there are convenient shelves and telescoping wall lamps in gilt bronze. The expedient of putting the bedroom in a closet, so to speak, made the arrangement of the living room easier to plan. The sloping walls under the roof dominate the room and have been used to best advantage. Green satin curtains, following the slope, are held in place by tiebacks. An English mahogany desk stands between two windows in a space that would otherwise be wasted. A pair of Directoire chairs on either side of a round table make a conversation group under one window, and under the other an overstuffed armchair near the built-in bookshelves makes an ideal reading corner. Another similar chair and a matching sofa complete the arrangement. The chairs and the sofa are covered in an old gold satin that introduces a note of luxury worthy of Louis XIV, while the deep wall-to-wall carpeting expresses the modern concept of comfort. The soft colors of the landscape by Guillaumin and the brilliant enamel of the Ming vase on the coffee table contribute greatly to the beauty of the setting.

AN APPARTMENT IN THE ROUND
Four rooms on four levels.

Mme. Malatier is a decorator, and when it came to decorating her own home she had no interest in creating her thirtieth Louis XIV living room or her fortieth Empire décor. Instead, she followed a spiral principle in arranging the space in her apartment. A sumptuous curving staircase links the various rooms from the living room to her bedroom. A few steps further up is the kitchen, created by borrowing a little space from the bedroom and by hiding a short service stair. The highest room in the apartment is the dining room, from which guests can look down on the scene much as diners do at Orly airport. With this background, the decoration had to be unorthodox, and Mme. Malatier knew how to achieve this with distinction. It is hard to say if the result is traditional or modern. What could be more contemporary than a dining room whose walls and ceiling are entirely covered with a straw-colored Japanese fiber paper? What idea could possibly be more typical of modern design (imported from America) than the raised fireplace with its massive white surround? Yet the warm familiarity of tradition is here, too, in the angled sofa loaded with cushions and in the Louis XVI panelled doors on the built-in cupboards that make up the walls of the bedroom. Thus the best of both worlds are delightfully combined in an apartment where the shortest distance between any two given points is never a straight line.

▲
From the bedroom, three of the apartment's four levels are visible: the bedroom level, the level of the dining room with its curved railing, and the living room level on the "ground floor". Notice how the architectural lines of the apartment are ingeniously emphasized. A grasscloth ceiling over the ▶ sofa underlines the curve of the balcony. On the fireplace wall, the same grasscloth makes a stunning contrast with the white mantelpiece. The lower step of the raised fireplace is strewn with cushions matching those on the sofa, and because of the width of the steps, they are at a comfortable distance from the fire.

Underneath the balcony, the ▶ ▶ angled sofa is one of the two main conversation areas in the room. The profusion of cushions and books gives it a cozy, intimate air.

Just two steps from the dining balcony, the compact kitchen was created from borrowed bedroom space. Lozenge tiles — orange on the floor and green on the walls — are the room's principal decoration.

▲
The bathroom is next to the bedroom. The "Pompeian amphorae" tiling in a pale gray shade covers the floor and part of the walls. The fixtures are all Idéal-Standard.

◄ Cupboards are the main decoration in the bedroom. Mme. Malatier put them on every wall, and the result looks more like panelling than useful storage space. They even run over the head of the bed to create a typically 18th-century alcove. The delicate white molding stands out against a banana-yellow background. The floor is covered with soft and soothing gray wall-to-wall carpeting.

◄ Striated wall covering, a variety of fabrics, books, and pictures, create a play of nuances in this unusual decorating scheme. The grasscloth that gives a feeling of lightness to the dining balcony seems to flow down into the living room on the lower level. The white areas of the balcony and the fireplace wall heighten the subtle shade of the grasscloth. Major accents are the red cushions and the Chinese red lacquer table.

The bench arranged ► like a banquette along the wall places seated guests where they have the best view of the living room below them. Twelve people can be seated at this table.

FOUR ROOMS ON FOUR LEVELS

IN TWO SERVANTS' ROOMS
A remarkable metamorphosis

In the rue Caumartin, on the sixth floor, is an apartment belonging to M. and Mme. Dupleix. There were formerly two servants' rooms here, under the eaves, with very little space and sloping walls caused by the mansard roof. To refurbish these rooms looked like a hopeless problem, but decorator Maurice Cabrol proved that even this metamorphosis was possible, for he either exploited or hid the basic obstacles that faced him. To make the rooms seem bigger than they are, he used cove ceilings, with the recessed area painted white. This construction had the added advantage of hiding an awkward soffit. To reduce the need for heavy pieces of furniture, he used built-in storage extensively — a cupboard tucked away, and, in a desk, a turntable. Horizontals were stressed everywhere — in the desk, in the bookcase, in the sofa, and even in the cove ceiling — while strong vertical lines were avoided in order to make the most of the available space. Finally, solid-colored materials were chosen with interesting textures such as the grain of wood and the roughness of grasscloth. These modern materials have an air of warmth and comfort that makes the apartment a simple and pleasant place in which to live.

The living room can easily be transformed into a dining room or a study. The walls are covered in a Japanese grasscloth wallpaper from **Nobilis**, which, with the toast wall-to-wall carpeting, makes a warm and restful background. The radiator is concealed beneath the bookshelves, and the desk (left) opens to reveal a turntable and a radio. The bar (above) merely seems to be a decorative detail with its big doors covered with a photographic mural. Plastic has been used as a lining for the bookshelves and to cover the door, which has thus been made impervious to fingerprints.

Limited space dictated the plan of the bathroom. The radiator is set into the side of the bathtub, and a towel rack makes it possible to keep towels warm and dry. A dressing table is fitted in underneath the washbasin, and it is raised slightly to make toe space at the bottom. A large mirror doubles the precious space optically, and the black slate lining to the bathtub alcove makes it appear unusually deep. The coated wallpaper design of cool, green, interlacing vines further contributes to the illusion.

The bedroom follows the decorating theme of the living room in a more subdued fashion. The cove ceiling and the carpeting are the same as in the living room, but the grass-cloth wallpaper has a more restful brick-red tone. The built-in storage unit was made to fit round the jogs of the mansard roof. It is a simple design in wood and painted white with light molding as decoration. The headboard and the backs of the night tables are caned.

After meals, the oiled Brazilian rosewood table by **Formes Nouvelles** is set at its lower position with its leaves folded back. Guests can sit on the black ottomans covered in Shaï or on the shaggy wool sofa that hides additional storage space. The raised fireplace is the focal point here. Its sides and top are of laminated olive wood, and the firebox is lined with firebrick painted black in contrast to the old gold satin curtains by **Frey**.

IN TWO SERVANTS' ROOMS *continued*

AN AMERICAN IN PARIS
Elegance and originality combined

The owner of this apartment appreciates comfort and an elegant kind of simplicity and is extremely nostalgic about his native land. The apartment he found under the eaves appealed to him precisely because it had no particular style, and in such a setting he was able to use furnishings and ornaments from many different periods. The corduroy-covered walls and the wall-to-wall carpeting make a neutral background against which unexpected pieces of furniture stand out with great effect: an armchair composed of horns, a huge American eagle, a framed flag that is not only colorful but also historic. Convenient cupboards are built into the embrasure of the door. The ornaments are deliberately simple: mirrors with 19th-century gesso frames, rows of prints, and one or two fine pieces of furniture without ormolu. The rooms have the welcoming charm of a real home where one can linger with pleasure among objects that are familiar rather than merely beautiful. The decoration here was by Pierre Madel.

◄ **A mixture of styles is apparent throughout. In the front hall, a 17th-century bronze equestrian figure stands between two covered Chinese vases on a Second Empire mantelpiece. Near the living-room door stands a Louis XVI mahogany chest of drawers, and the threshold is covered with a small American gros-point rug. The living room contains elegant ornaments such as the marble bust set between a pair of Louis XV candlesticks. The comfortable armchair by the blazing hearth, the wall-to-wall carpeting, and the walls covered with rep give a feeling of coziness and warmth.**

An ingenious arrangement makes it possible to spend more time than usual in a room that is often ignored — the front hall — for here it does double duty as a dining room. This explains the furniture, which plays a double role too: a table displaying fine bibelots is used as a dining table, and a chest of drawers serves as a sideboard.

The desire for comfort inspired the decoration of the bedroom, which is ► a panelled retreat just off the living room. The high row of cupboards is hardly noticeable under the teak doors. The American flag (its thirty-seven stars date it at 1867) and the cushions covered in petit-point tapestry give a distinctive character to the simple decorating scheme.

AN AMERICAN IN PARIS *continued*

◄ The living room is a room of many moods. The sofa, which is covered in a corduroy of the same color as the walls and floor, discreetly invites one to sit down and relax beneath the impressive American eagle. The Transition chest of drawers (below left) is surmounted by a clock and a pair of Louis XV sconces to produce a scene of 18th-century elegance. A piano (below right) and modern paintings give a more personal look to their corner of the room. ▼

PROBLEMS
AND SOLUTIONS

A hundred questions and a thousand minor obstacles seem to crop up during redecorating and remodeling jobs. Here, in no particular order, are some typical problems and their solutions. In each legend the letter "P" signifies "problem" and "S" "solution."

◄ **P. How to fit a bedroom and a study into the same room. S. You can hang a platform from metal scaffolding rods secured to the ceiling. Here the desk top is a specially treated slab of glass set on a framework fastened into the wall. A wall of built-in cupboards with doors covered with mahogany and pine panels solves the bedroom storage problem.**

P. How do you divide up a large open space decorated in the classic manner, without cutting one room completely off from the other? S. Decorator Victor Grandpierre devised this double door. When both doors are closed, the entire doorway slides back on tracks into the walls at either side. See pages 34-37 for other pictures of this apartment.

PROBLEMS AND SOLUTIONS

▲
P. Mme. Mondovi wanted to counteract the narrowness of her kitchen and the smallness of the floor. S. She chose a tiled floor depicting a hunting scene. The original design is in the Musée de la Vénerie at Senlis.

P. How do you make a garden seem like part of a room? S. Architect Jacques Fildier opened up his outside wall by using two large sliding panes of glass and a third fixed pane. Then he covered the floor with the same pattern of green marble pebbles used on the terrace outside.

P. To shelter a terrace that was an extension of a very low house. S. Decorator Pierre Duchier stretched canvas over a framework of tubing supported by metal posts, and he gave it a gentle slope so that it would shed rain.

P. The work you do involves ▶ research and it would be convenient to be able to consult books and magazines at the same time. **S.** Adopt sloping shelves supported by metal uprights, which can also support flat shelves.

P. How to make metal filing cabinets look more attractive in your study. **S.** Sheathe them with wood and build bookshelves above them at the same time.
▼
P. How to cut down on the extra leg work that ironing demands. **S.** Fix the ironing board on a pivot in a shallow closet, as demonstrated here.

P. You would like a convenient way of finding the pair of gloves you want. **S.** Hang a series of large brass rings near the front door.

P. What can one do with a long tele- ▶ phone cord when the phone is sometimes needed in different parts of the room? **S.** Roll it up on a reel attached ot the bottom of a shelf, as architect André Svetchine has done. This avoids a permanent tangle of cords.

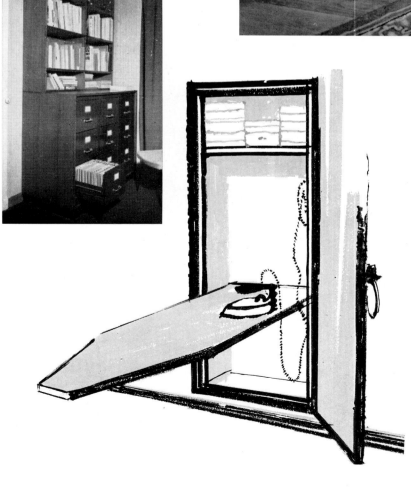

PROBLEMS AND SOLUTIONS

▲
P. Where can a home movie screen be hidden? **S.** Leleu hid it behind a tapestry mounted on a triangle that has one arm hinged on the wall.

▲
P. How can curtains be fixed so that they can be taken down to be cleaned and put up again without the usual gymnastics? **S.** Use a smooth teak rod and hang the curtain from large loops of braid closed with snaps.

▲
P. How do you disguise a medicine chest? **S.** By making it a display area for plaster moldings.

▲
P. You would love to have a greenhouse for some exotic plants without going to too much expense. **S.** Cut through the wall and close the opening with a bay or double set of windows.

◄ **P.** You need an absolutely skidproof surface on your driveway, which has a steep slope. **S.** Bricks laid in a herringbone pattern are an effective and attractive answer.

P. You want evenly distributed light in your kitchen. S. The luminous path of plastic tiles as arranged by Maurice Cabrol. The advantages: they soften the light, distribute it evenly and collect little condensation.

P. You have only a narrow space in which to build a staircase. S. Steps set at angles. The advantage: it's more secure than a ladder.

P. The cushions of the banquettes in your chalet always slip out of place. S. One long, single cushion can be held in place by loops that fit over hooks screwed in the wall.

P. You need shelves ▶ for large items like skis and camping equipment. S. A false ceiling of tongue-and-groove planks with hinges.

P. A jutting rock ▶ is on the site of the house you plan. S. The supporting wall can rest directly on the rock.

P. You have to hide a network of pipes. S. The prismatic ceiling of plaster board by architect Italo Ferrari hid pipes and the reinforced concrete ceiling of this basement room in Lausanne.

PROBLEMS AND SOLUTIONS

297

P. There are too many doors in the front hall. **S.** One way of disguising them is by superimposing a shallow cabinet, like this one by Raoul Guiraud, fitted into the top panel of the door. Inside the glass front is a display of bibelots.

P. Cupboards on every wall can seem like a Kafka nightmare. **S.** Sliding doors divided into panels can be used as frames. On the doors of this linen closet, burnished steel moldings, strong enough to make a framework, bracket the pages of a medieval hymnal. The pages are covered by glass, of course.

P. Where can one hide the bathroom hot water heater when the bathroom itself is too small? **S.** Pierre Barbe had a unique answer. He put the heater in a cupboard over his shirt drawers. A separate door hides it even when the cupboard is open.

▲ **P.** You have a phobia about tarnished silver. **S.** Line the inside of the silver cupboard door with an impregnated cloth that will inhibit tarnishing. And why not display the flat silver like a collection so that you can easily keep count of it?

◄ **P. A hallway lined ►** with utilitarian cupboards and drawers is depressing, but there is nowhere else to put them. **S.** Here chintz covers the flaps of drawers which have hidden hinges and magnetic catches. With the flaps closed, they seem to disappear into the chintz wall, since small brass knobs are all that is needed to open the drawers.

PROBLEMS AND SOLUTIONS

P. How to make do without a cupboard for tableware. S. Curt Jurgens devised a heavy tabletop with two hinged faps that give access to a long trough hidden under the table. The trough itself is mounted on casters so that it can be rolled into the kitchen to collect clean dishes.

P. A baby's playpen is always in the way when not in use. **S. A** niche in the wall will hold it. Later on, toys can be stored in the niche with cabinet doors to close it off.

P. How to conceal a radiator without taking up usable space. **S.** Why not put it in a linen closet and make the lower panel of the door a grille.

P. How to substitute a mirror for a window and still retain an opening. **S.** Architect Jacques Regnault replaced the window pane with a mirror surrounded with clear glass that still lets in the light.

▼

P. Do individual dressing rooms for ▶ swimmers, huntsmen, or other sportsmen have to spoil a hall or washroom? **S.** Not if they have multicolored portières hanging at the entrance to each cubicle to give them the look of theatre boxes.

P. Collectors of old tools like to ▶ see them displayed. **S. A** happy answer is to arrange them on a panel of velvet in the manner of a still life and frame them for the wall.

P. Cookbooks soil too easily in the kitchen. **S. A** hanging lectern keeps them visible but off the counter.

P. Sloping walls create such awkward corners. **S. Consider** building cupboards or drawers as here into the lower part of the wall.

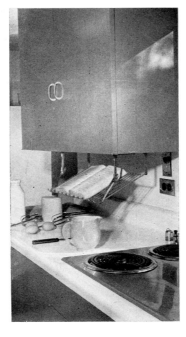

PROBLEMS AND SOLUTIONS

PROBLEMS AND SOLUTIONS

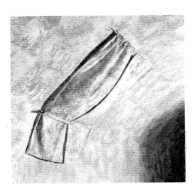

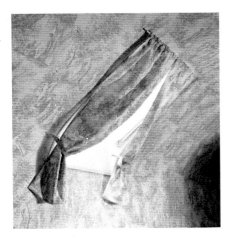

◀ P. Can the anachronism of a television set in an 18th-century décor be avoided? S. The best answer is to build the receiver into the wall and cover it. Here, Fred de Cabrol masks it with a painting. The frame slides up into the wall on tracks when the TV is to be used.

◀ P. In many old houses there are bare pipes that can ruin the look of a room. S. Box them in or enclose them in panelling to make a modern storage wall. The space not occupied by pipes can be used to display books or bibelots.

P. To hide a projection room in a study. S. The Vincenot studio devised a large wooden panel on hinges that pivots to reveal the screen. The projector is tucked away in a cupboard. Amplifiers hidden behind curtains in the corners of the window embrasures transmit the ◀ host's commentaries.

▲

P. Dressing up a skylight with curtains is an awkward operation. S. Here two elastic tiebacks fitted with clasps keep the curtains against the sloping wall at all times.

P. The accepted theory is that valances ▶ are incompatible with exposed beams, especially in a low-ceilinged room. S. A cut-out valance fitting snugly around the beams can make a fine exception to the rule.

P. Radiators are out of place in an ele- ▶ gant décor. S. When remodeling, have the radiators set into the walls and install flaps that open on either side of the panel to let the heat into the room. These flaps fold back against the curtains to protect them from dust.

P. Kitchen stairs are often poky and ▶ unattractive looking. S. They can be painted in gay colors or fitted with tiles. Here Jacques Bouchardy used blue tiles set into the plain white tiles of the stair risers.

P. What to do about curtains when the ▶ window runs right up to the top of the embrasure? S. In this bathroom, the rods pivot so that the curtains can be opened and closed like shutters.

303

▲
◀ **P.** You have chosen a modern country style décor and find that traditional doors look out of place, yet you wish to close off the hall that leads to the kitchen. **S.** Short, shuttered, swinging doors, inspired by the saloons of the Old West.

P. There is no hall or reception room between the stair landing and your office. **S.** Here the landing door was enclosed with a frame that includes a second door — all made out of the same wood as the furniture. This solution has the added advantage of sound-proofing the office.

P. You would like to be able to ▶ keep an eye on the children while they are in the playroom. **S.** A Dutch door will keep the children in and visible. Notice that the latches here are on the parents' side of the door.

P. There is no room for an outside ▶ door as well as a picture window, but you still want easy access to the garden. **S.** A glass panel, like this one designed by architect Jacques Bouchardy, that pivots on a central axis and carries its curtains along with it.

P. Husbands and wives do not always read in bed until the same hour. **S.** A flat folding screen or door fitted in between the twin beds can make two rooms out of one. This one disappears into the wall, leaving only the track visible.

PROBLEMS AND SOLUTIONS

17TH CENTURY

Few pieces of domestic French furniture from the Renaissance or earlier are suitable for interior decoration today. In France, the earliest pieces usually used are those dating back to Louis XIII. At that time Spanish and Dutch influences were rife, but a typically French style was in the process of development. In the provinces, the shapes, designs, and ornamentation first seen in the 17th century have persisted in country pieces right down to the present day. So anyone planning to remodel a country house in the French style might do well to turn to the 17th-century style for inspiration.

BUFFET WITH TURNED PILASTERS

TABLE WITH STRETCHERS AND TURNED LEGS

STOOL WITH CONSOLE LEGS

**BRASS CANDLESTICK
WITH A LARGE SQUARE BASE**

BEVELED MIRROR WITH BRASS AND TORTOISE-SHELL FRAME

**ARMCHAIR WITH STRETCHERS AND
TYPICALLY LOUIS XIII ARMS**

GLOSSARY
OF STYLES

LOUIS XIV

This period was rich in architectural display and decorative ideas. The pieces of furniture that already existed were improved in both comfort and elegance, and new pieces such as the bergère, the sofa, the daybed, the chest of drawers, and the console table were introduced. Ornamentation was increasingly refined, but it was always in proportion to the structure of the piece. The furniture ordered for the court of "Le Roi Soleil" was lavishly ornamented, either carved and gilded or made of ebony inlaid with pewter, brass, or tortoise shell in the style of Boulle. The ordinary domestic furniture, made of walnut, suits present-day interiors very well. At the end of the reign, the Régence style made its appearance — suppler and more graceful, leading directly to Louis XV.

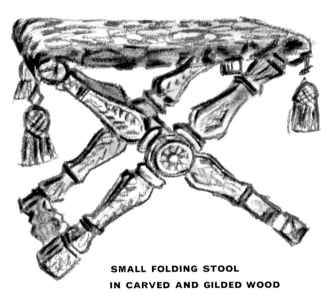

SMALL FOLDING STOOL IN CARVED AND GILDED WOOD

MIRROR FRAMED IN GILT BRONZE WITH A MASK

LATE LOUIS XIV ARMCHAIR WITH SEAT AND BACK BORDERED IN WOOD

MARQUETRY TABLE OF TORTOISE SHELL AND BRASS BY A. C. BOULLE AFTER A DESIGN BY BÉRAIN

THE LOWBOY CAME INTO USE AT THIS TIME

LOUIS XV

The suppleness and gaiety of furniture designed with curves and reverse curves reflected the spirit of the court in the reign of Louis XV. Cabinetwork and bronze-casting reached a peak of perfection, and for the first time signed pieces were made. Exotic woods were used for marquetry, and mahogany made its appearance together with walnut and oak. Sculptured ornamentation, in shallower relief than in the previous reign, was now asymmetric, busy, and full of delightful surprises. Even the everyday furniture of the period, with its simple outlines, was graceful, and such pieces fit happily into the decoration and way of life of our own times.

BERGÈRE IN CARVED AND GILDED WOOD

ARMCHAIR FOR HAIRDRESSING

GAMING TABLE OF BLOND WOOD AND MAHOGANY

CHAIR WITH CANING AND MOLDING — A POPULAR PIECE ▶

ROCOCO SCONCE

GILT BRONZE KEYHOLE ESCUTCHEONS

SCREEN-WRITING DESK IN VIOLET WOOD WITH DAMASK SCREEN

BOUDOIR CHAIR BY GEORGES JACOB
BELONGING TO THE QUEEN

A CANDELABRUM AND A SÈVRES VASE
WITH A GILT BRONZE MOUNT

ANOTHER JACOB CHAIR, CARVED AND LACQUERED

LOUIS XVI

A reaction now set in and the sinuous lines of the preceding style went out of favor. Designs were straightforward, symmetrical, rectilinear; and wood carving was often reduced to beading, foliage, and medallions. Bronzes were lighter and less frequently seen. Furniture painted in light colors began to appear. Mahogany was the most popular wood, and really fine furniture had inlays of precious materials. Despite the influence of the styles uncovered at Pompeii, the furniture of this period kept its purely French character, and it is very much in favor throughout the world today.

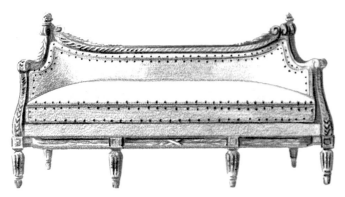

RICHLY CARVED GILT SOFA WITH SIX FEET

CANED CHAIR
WITH A CURVED SPINDLE BACK

A LADY'S WRITING DESK

BEDSIDE TABLE: TRANSITION BETWEEN
LOUIS XV AND LOUIS XVI

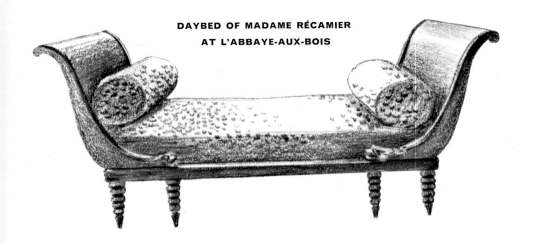

DAYBED OF MADAME RÉCAMIER
AT L'ABBAYE-AUX-BOIS

ARMCHAIR WITH
SPHINX-HEAD ARMS

DIRECTOIRE

After the Revolution, the artisans of Paris went back to work and created a style that emphasized lightness and made increasing use of the linear pattern introduced in the time of Louis XVI. The fashion now was for open chair-backs, scrolls and palm fronds, lions' feet, and supports with carved Egyptian heads. Since the disruption of commerce, mahogany was hard to obtain and fruitwood became more popular. The examples seen here, signed by Jacob Frères, rue Meslée, were made between 1796 and 1803.

WALL SCONCE
IN BLACK AND GILT BRONZE

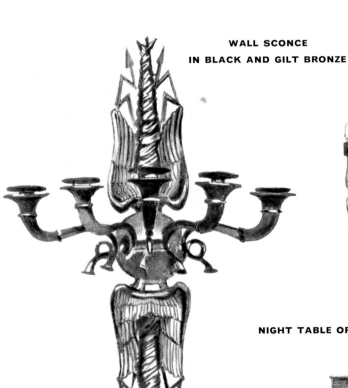

ROUND TABLE OF MAHOGANY AND MOSAIC
ON BRONZE FEET

OPEN-BACK SIDE CHAIR

NIGHT TABLE OF MAHOGANY, LEMONWOOD, AND GILT BRONZE

MAHOGANY CONSOLE WITH HIND'S FEET

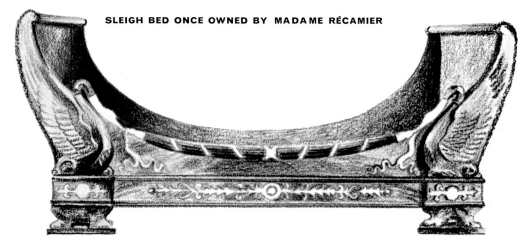

SLEIGH BED ONCE OWNED BY MADAME RÉCAMIER

CHEVAL-GLASS WITH GILT BRONZE CARYATIDS

EMPIRE

Inspired by ancient Rome rather than Greece, the sometimes heavy Empire furniture was a conscious reflection of the official pomp of Napoleon's court. But it was not without a certain perfection of design and workmanship, and today's decorators have found new ways to use Empire pieces with exciting results. Mahogany was the favored wood, and gilt bronze ornamentation was typical. The best examples of this style were made by Thomire. In the provinces, the city styles were copied in local wood and then stained to look like mahogany. All the examples on this page are signed Jacob-Desmalter, who was active from 1803 to 1824.

BRONZE HANGING CLOCK
WITH MARTIAL EAGLE

ROUND TABLE
WITH MARBLE AND WOOD TOP

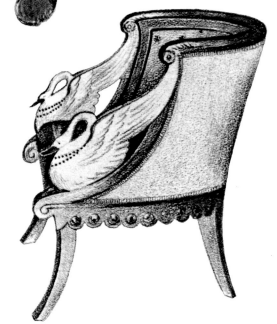

MAHOGANY AND GILT BRONZE
SECRETARY

MADAME RÉCAMIER'S
ALTAR-SHAPED NIGHT TABLE

GILT WOOD ARMCHAIR MADE FOR SAINT-CLOUD

RESTORATION

Returning exiles rejected the ideas of the Empire period. In the midst of this sudden change, decoration sought its inspiration not in the classic age but rather in the Middle Ages, and there was a brief fashion for Gothic revival. Simultaneously, a new romanticism developed under the influence of the Duchesse de Berry and found expression in charming blond wood furniture. Even so, it was impossible to escape entirely from shapes that had by now become familiar, and many Restoration pieces betray Empire influence, although lightened and softened. Later, under Louis Philippe, mahogany came back into fashion, and heavier furniture appeared once more. The pieces shown here are all by A. Jacob Fs & Cie.

SIDEBOARD IN GRAINED MAPLE WITH PAINTED GLASS DOOR PANELS

ROUND MAHOGANY TABLE MADE FOR LOUIS PHILIPPE

GONDOLA CHAIR WITH SIMULATED BAMBOO

GRACEFUL CHAIR OF LEMONWOOD AND AMARANTH

GILT BRONZE TIEBACKS

SMALL BIRD'S-EYE MAPLE COUCH

ARMCHAIR IN LEMONWOOD AND MAPLE

STOOL WITH GILT FEET IN ROPEWORK DESIGN

**GONDOLA CHAIR
WITH A HANDLE ON THE BACK**

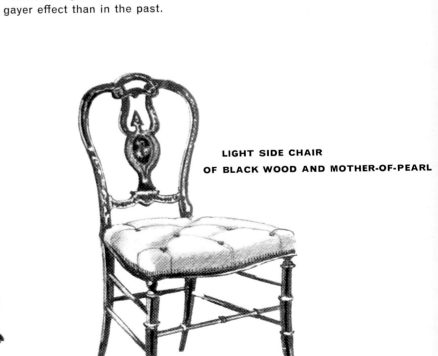

**BEVELED MIRROR WITH
A *VERRE ÉGLOMISÉ* FRAME**

NAPOLEON III

During this twenty-year period many large fortunes were made owing to industrial growth, the railroads, and the rebuilding of Paris. The new vogue for luxurious furniture took its inspiration from many periods, but the main themes were Louis XV and Venetian. Overstuffed upholstery hid the cabinetwork of armchairs and sofas, fabrics were overloaded with designs, as were carpets, wallpapers, and marquetry. The rich effect and comfort of the style is still admired today, and elements of Napoleon III are often found in good contemporary decoration, though refined and refurbished to give rooms a lighter and gayer effect than in the past.

**BLACK LACQUER WRITING DESK
INLAID WITH MOTHER-OF-PEARL**

OVERSTUFFED "BORNE"

**LIGHT SIDE CHAIR
OF BLACK WOOD AND MOTHER-OF-PEARL**

ENGLISH STYLES

LOWBOY WITH CABRIOLE LEGS

CARVED SHELL — A TYPICAL MOTIF

SECRETARY SHOWING DUTCH INFLUENCE

Queen Anne

The last Stuart sovereign reigned from 1702 to 1714, and great architects such as Wren, Vanbrugh, and Kent were responsible for the interior decoration of the magnificent houses they built for the new aristocracy. The furniture designed by these men gave English pieces an architectural imprint. Walnut, ornamented with floral marquetry, was a popular survival from previous reigns.

Chippendale

The London cabinetmaker Thomas Chippendale set the style for the years 1741 to 1760. During his long career Chippendale created many new shapes and motifs, borrowing details and inspiration from Portuguese, Gothic, Chinese, and French sources. He limited himself to mahogany and used the wood for vigorous carved ornamentation.

BOOKCASE WITH CRISSCROSSED MUNTINS

GOTHIC-BACKED CHAIR

THREE-TIERED TABLE

Hepplewhite and Sheraton

The golden age of arts and crafts began around 1780 with the works of Hepplewhite. His lightly scaled pieces in faultless taste were sometimes painted, sometimes inlaid with light-colored woods. In 1791 Thomas Sheraton published a remarkable book of designs which showed his ability to carry the feeling of lightness to its extreme. He dispensed with carving and made much use of mahogany veneers and inlays.

SHERATON DRAWER PULLS

SHERATON LIBRARY TABLE

PAINTED HEPPLEWHITE ARMCHAIR

Regency

The Regency style — which is not to be confused with the Régence style in France — flourished during the first twenty years of the 19th century. Two of its major practitioners were the architects Thomas Hope and Henry Holland. New woods — rosewood, ebony, Amboyna, and Coromandel — replaced mahogany. The furniture of this period is small-scaled, but the dark surfaces sparkle with delicate moldings and brass or gilt-bronze inlays. Today, in London, the handsome furniture of this period is much sought after by connoisseurs and decorators because it combines easily with contemporary décor.

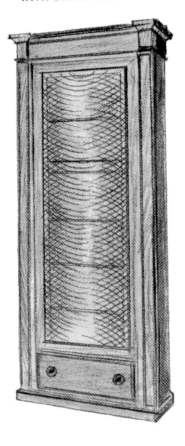

**BOOKCASE
WITH BRASS GRILLE**

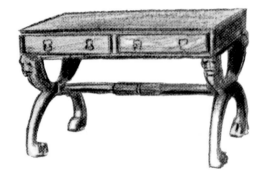

TYPICAL LIONS' HEADS AND FEET

GIRANDOLE MIRROR WITH GILDED WOOD FRAME

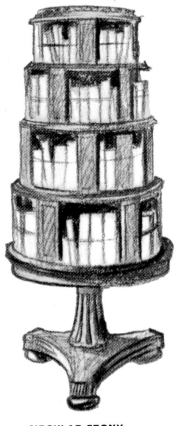

**CIRCULAR EBONY
BOOKSTAND WITH
REVOLVING SHELVES**

Early Victorian

After the effervescence of Regency, there was a return to the solid virtues of massive mahogany and rosewood. Some designs taken from Sheraton's posthumous book were much copied but almost always given a more robust character. Other designs reflect the romanticism of Sir Walter Scott. But the industrial revolution gave a new direction to design by changing manufacturing methods. Wood turned on a lathe appeared, and the Crystal Palace Exhibition of 1851 gave an impetus to mass production, thus precipitating the decline of craftsmanship in English furniture design.

CARVED MAHOGANY WINE COOLER

MAHOGANY AND VELVET UPHOLSTERED CHAIR

**DETAIL OF
A TABLE LEG:
UPSIDE-DOWN LOTUS LEAF**

**A WHATNOT
OF TURNED WOOD**

INDEX
by subject

INDEX continued

Index of owners

Index of artists

Photos by **Frank Beyda** appear on pages 141, 224-225, 230-241, 244-245, 254-257, 268-275, 286-289, 304.

Index of decorators, architects, landscape architects

The printing of this book

was completed on January 25th, 1967

by l'Imprimerie Kapp

at Vanves-92

and l'Imprimerie Sapho at Bobigny-93

PRINTED IN FRANCE

PRINTER N° 7785